FIREWORKS MX
MAGIC

Lisa Lopuck

 New Riders

www.newriders.com
201 West 103rd Street, Indianapolis, Indiana 46290
An imprint of Pearson Education
Boston • Indianapolis • London • Munich • New York • San Francisco

FIREWORKS MX MAGIC

International Standard Book Number: 0-7357-1140-2

Library of Congress Catalog Card Number: 20-01088188

Printed in the United States of America

05 04 03 02   7 6 5 4 3 2 1

Interpretation of the printing code: The rightmost double-digit number is the year of the book's printing; the rightmost single-digit number is the number of the book's printing. For example, the printing code 02-1 shows that the first printing of the book occurred in 2002.

Trademarks

Warning and Disclaimer

Publisher
David Dwyer

Associate Publisher
Stephanie Wall

Managing Editor
Kristy Knoop

Acquisitions Editors
Linda Anne Bump
Elise Walter

Development Editor
Ginny Bess Munroe

Product Marketing Manager
Kathy Malmloff

Publicity Manager
Susan Nixon

Project Editor
Suzanne Pettypiece

Copy Editor
Amy Lepore

Indexer
Chris Morris

Manufacturing Coordinator
Jim Conway

Cover Designer
Aren Howell

Proofreader
Sarah Cisco

Composition
Ron Wise

Media Developer
Jay Payne

ABOUT THE AUTHORS

Lisa Lopuck

Lisa Lopuck is an award-winning web designer, a highly regarded speaker at web conferences around the world, and a best-selling author. She has been on Macromedia's Fireworks advisory board since the product's inception and for the last 10 years has consulted as web creative strategist for numerous high-profile companies including eBay, Inktomi, Palm, Sprint, National Geographic, Twentieth Century Fox, Microsoft, and Apple. She was the founder and Chief Creative Officer of eHandsOn.com, an online learning company, and in 1996 was cofounder and Creative Director of the award-winning web design firm Electravision. Lopuck holds a bachelor of arts in communication design from UCLA.

Jeffrey Bardzell

Jeffrey Bardzell is an e-learning specialist at Indiana University. He also is a Macromedia software trainer and author, e-learning consultant, occasional literature instructor, and former education policy analyst. His computer publications include *Special Edition Using Fireworks MX* (Que Publishing, August 2002, ISBN: 0789727269), *Fireworks 4 Expert Edge* (McGraw-Hill/Osborne, July 2001 ISBN: 0072131462), *Flash 5: An Architectural Approach* (an online curriculum at eHandsOn), and contributions to the *Flash 5 Bible* (Hungry Minds, Inc., February 2001, ISBN: 0764535153). His academic publications include *Improving Early Reading and Literacy* (Corwin, forthcoming) as well as several articles on early literacy, school finance reform, and epic poetry.

Joyce J. Evans

Joyce Evans has more than 10 years of experience in educational teaching, tutorial development, and web design. She has received Editors' Choice awards for her *Fireworks 4 f/x & Design* book (The Coriolis Group, May 2001, ISBN: 1576109968) and has authored numerous graphic design titles including *Dreamweaver MX Complete Course* (Hungry Minds, Inc., September 2002, ISBN: 0764536869). She also has contributed to several books such as *Dreamweaver 4: The Complete Reference* (McGraw-Hill/Osborne, May 2001, ISBN: 0072131713) and *Dreamweaver MX/Fireworks MX Savvy* (Sybex, May 2002, 0782141110). Joyce actively writes reviews and articles for several graphic design magazines.

Steven Grosvenor

Steven Grosvenor is cofounder of **www.phireworx.com**, a Fireworks resource site, coauthor of *Dreamweaver MX Expert Edge* (McGraw-Hill/Osborne, July 2002, ISBN: 0072223553) and is Senior Systems Architect for a managed Internet security company in the United Kingdom. Grosvenor's background is in cross-platform systems integration, interface design, and interaction and architecture design. Demand from users for a customized, interactive experience led him to develop and create many timesaving and creative commands and behaviors for Dreamweaver, vastly reducing deployment time for corporate sites and increasing their portability and scalability. His drive to increase team productivity led him to develop extensibility add-ons for other products in the Macromedia web suite including Dreamweaver MX, Fireworks MX, and Flash MX. One of the new breeds of commands for Fireworks MX, "Twist and Fade 3.0," created by Grosvenor, had the accolade of shipping with Fireworks MX. His other publications include several Fireworks MX and Dreamweaver MX tutorials, which can be found at **www.macromedia.com**.

Joe Marini

Joe Marini received his bachelor of science degree in computer engineering technology from the Rochester Institute of Technology in 1991. He has been developing software professionally for 15 years for companies such as Quark, mFactory, and Macromedia, and he was a founding partner of his own company, Lepton Technologies. While at Macromedia, Marini was an original member of the Dreamweaver development team and represented the company at the W3C's DOM Working Group. Marini lives and works in San Francisco, California, with his wife, Stacy, and dog, Milo.

Abigail Rudner

Abigail Rudner is an artist, designer, trainer, and consultant specializing in web and interface design and photo illustration. She has worked with clients including Levi's, Wells Fargo, *The Wall Street Journal*, America Online, Absolute Vodka, Apple, Microsoft, *FAD* and *Publish!* Magazines. She has taught web design and related topics with love and enthusiasm across the United States for the better part of 10 years. Rudner holds a bachelor of fine arts from Parsons School of Design.

Anne-Marie Yerks

Ann-Marie Yerks is an author, instructor, and fine artist from Ann Arbor, Michigan. She recently worked with New Riders Publishing as lead author of *Inside Dreamweaver 4* (ISBN: 0735710848), which was published in May 2001. Yerks also has developed online classes for New York University's virtual campus, for Sessions.edu, and has taught web design at George Washington University. She began working with Fireworks several years ago in her job as a web developer for the *Journal of Commerce*. She also has worked on web sites for PBS, the Environmental Protection Agency, and the University of Michigan, and she has contributed to a variety of books and publications, including *Web Review*, *Intranets Unleashed*, and Lycos.com.

ABOUT THE TECHNICAL REVIEWERS

These reviewers contributed their considerable hands-on expertise to the entire development process for *Fireworks MX Magic*. As the book was being written, these dedicated professionals reviewed all the material for technical content, organization, and flow. Their feedback was critical to ensuring that *Fireworks MX Magic* fits our reader's need for the highest-quality technical information.

Marc Garrett

Marc Garrett began building web sites in 1996. Among his many projects, he has helped Northeast Historic Film lay the foundations of a digital media archive, has developed applications for Blue Circle North America's intranet, and has built an online store for Pegasus Communications. Garrett also contributes reviews and interviews to his own web site, **www.since1968.com**. In his quiet moments, he suspects he may have missed his calling as a snake handler and wonders if it's not too late.

Eric R. Infanti

Eric Infanti (CIW, CI), an author, trainer, and web coach, expresses his passion through creative technical writing, a positive training style, and innovative web design. Infanti is an award-winning certified Internet webmaster and certified instructor and is the Chief Web Designer and Director of Training and Performance for a Connecticut-based design and training firm. Infanti also has more than 14 years of experience managing the conceptual design and information architecture for web/IT products and leads the philosophy and strategy of training initiatives, forming the nucleus of learning project teams, delivery of technology and management-centric certification courses, instructional design, and follow-through training evaluation and measurement methods. Infanti's web and design capacity has earned several awards, using tools such as Flash and LiveMotion to integrate media design and content usability methodology. He also is the principal designer and creator of **www.FlashTrainingDesign.com**, a tutorial and content guide on Flash used as an information design tool. Infanti has authored *Developing Web Sites with Flash 6* and *The Ten Minute Guide to Visio 2002* and has served as the technical editor for several books on topics such as Adobe Photoshop and Dreamweaver. He also delivers keynote lectures and training seminars nationally. Infanti can be reached at **Eric@FlashTrainingDesign.com**.

Mary Rich

Mary Rich began her career as an insurance agent. Rich made the switch to become a programming trainee, found out what programmers did, and fell in love! The affair continued through mainframes and midrange systems and then peaked when the first IBM-PCs arrived. Rich eventually got involved with various graphics programs and then web sites. A believer in Macromedia products, Rich found Dreamweaver and Fireworks to be the answer to her prayers for productivity. Rich provides consulting and training in many different areas to organizations in the Los Angeles, California area and—via the Internet—to the world. She has a bachelor of arts degree from Brown University and is working on a certificate in computer graphics from UCLA. Rich's cat, Friday, allows her to live with him in El Segundo, California.

Jeremy Wilson

Jeremy Wilson is a freelance web developer/web designer who hosts his own web design and development resource site, **www.jeremywilson.com**. Wilson's experience as a formally trained web designer has brought him to nationally recognized SAFECO Insurance, and prior to that he worked as a web developer (guide) with the Seattle design firm Digital Sherpas. Wilson is certified in Flash/ActionScript, Dreamweaver, and Fireworks technologies, recently adding certifications in JavaScript, Perl/CGI, and ASP/VBScript as well. Additionally, Wilson provides consulting, design, and development services to small and medium-size businesses in the Seattle, Washington area. Wilson holds a bachelor's degree from the University of Washington in communications (focusing on new media technologies) as well as a minor in Germanics, and he currently is working on a bachelor's degree in computer science. Wilson currently resides in Seattle, Washington, with his family, Trista and Alex.

DEDICATION

This book is dedicated to the many talented Fireworks authors and designers who helped make this a great book!

Jeffrey Bardzell

Donna Casey

Joyce J. Evans

Steven Grosvenor

Joe Marini

Abigail Rudner

Anne-Marie Yerks

TELL US WHAT YOU THINK

As the reader of this book, you are the most important critic and commentator. We value your opinion and want to know what we're doing right, what we could do better, in what areas you'd like to see us publish, and any other words of wisdom you're willing to pass our way.

As the Associate Publisher at New Riders Publishing, I welcome your comments. You can fax, email, or write me directly to let me know what you did or didn't like about this book—as well as what we can do to make our books stronger.

Please note that I cannot help you with technical problems related to the topic of this book, and that due to the high volume of mail I receive, I might not be able to reply to every message.

When you write, please be sure to include this book's title and author as well as your name and phone or fax number. I will carefully review your comments and share them with the author and editors who worked on the book.

Fax: 317-581-4663

Email: **stephanie.wall@newriders.com**

Mail: Stephanie Wall
         Associate Publisher
         New Riders Publishing
         201 West 103rd Street
         Indianapolis, IN 46290 USA

Visit Our Web Site: www.newriders.com

On our web site, you'll find information about our other books, the authors we partner with, book updates and file downloads, promotions, discussion boards for online interaction with other users and with technology experts, and a calendar of trade shows and other professional events with which we'll be involved. We hope to see you around.

Email Us from Our Web Site

Go to **www.newriders.com** and click on the Contact Us link if you

- Have comments or questions about this book.
- Want to report errors that you have found in this book.
- Have a book proposal or are interested in writing for New Riders.
- Would like us to send you one of our author kits.
- Are an expert in a computer topic or technology and are interested in being a reviewer or technical editor.
- Want to find a distributor for our titles in your area.
- Are an educator/instructor who wants to preview New Riders books for classroom use. In the body/comments area, include your name, school, department, address, phone number, office days/hours, text currently in use, and enrollment in your department, along with your request for either desk/examination copies or additional information.

INTRODUCTION

A few years ago, I used to be a hard-core Photoshop evangelist, user, and instructor. That all changed when I saw a demonstration of a fledgling web design product called Fireworks. As a professional web designer, illustrator, author, and instructor, I immediately recognized the brilliance of Fireworks. Finally, one product was specifically designed to address the needs of web designers.

To this day, Fireworks continues to evolve with features that enhance the web design and production workflow. Its vector and bitmap illustration capabilities rival those of other popular products. When you combine these with Fireworks's animation and interactive features, you have a world-class web design package.

In this book, I've brought together some of the most talented Fireworks users in the world to share with you their production techniques and shortcuts. The goal is to take you beyond the ranks of the casual Fireworks user and turn you into a power user so that you can integrate Fireworks into your professional life.

WHO WE ARE

The people who contributed to this book are a mix of tech heads and artsy folks. (I count myself as one of the latter.) I think that having such a varied mix of professional perspectives will help you identify with Fireworks. The idea is that even if you do not consider yourself an "artist," Fireworks still has so much to offer.

WHO YOU ARE

In writing this book, we assumed that you are a professional web designer who has toyed with Fireworks but has never used it for "paying" projects. You are clinging desperately to Photoshop for all your web design and production needs, but you are interested in learning whether Fireworks could fit into your workflow.

What's in This Book

This book contains step-by-step projects designed to give you practice with real-world Fireworks web design techniques. The projects cover everything from creating original art in Fireworks to building interactive web pages and integrating Fireworks with other programs such as Dreamweaver and Macromedia Flash.

The CD-ROM

Each project presented in this book has a project folder on the accompanying CD-ROM with all of the files and examples you'll need to follow along with the step-by-step instructions.

Our Assumptions as We Wrote This Book

The techniques and steps presented in this book assume that you are familiar with getting around either a Mac or a PC and have had prior experience with web graphics software such as Photoshop, Illustrator, Freehand, Dreamweaver, or Flash. In addition, you should have some working familiarity with Fireworks—even experience with earlier versions of the software. The projects are intermediate to advanced in their user level.

Conventions Used in This Book

Every computer book has its own style of presenting information. As you flip through the book, you'll notice that we have an interesting layout going on here. Because we know most of you are really into graphics, the project openers contain way-cool eye candy. The real meat of the projects starts on the next page. Take a look.

In the left column, you'll find step-by-step instructions for completing the project, as well as succinct but extremely valuable explanations. The text next to the number contains the action you must perform. In many cases, the action text is followed by a paragraph that contains contextual information. Note that if you want to perform the steps quickly and without any background info, you only need read the text next to the step numbers.

In the corresponding columns to the right, you'll find screen captions (and/or code) illustrating the steps. Code lines that break to the next line are noted with a code continuation character (➡). You'll also find Notes and Tips (in both columns) that will provide additional contextual information or customization techniques.

In the "Modifications" section at the end of each project, you'll find unique customization information. Each *Magic* project is designed to be highly customizable; therefore, we provide more tips and examples of what you can do with the techniques you've learned so that you can apply them to your own work quickly and easily.

UNBELIEVABLE VECTOR ILLUSTRATION

"There is no try, only do or do not."

—YODA IN *THE EMPIRE STRIKES BACK*

CREATING REALISTIC, BITMAP-LOOKING VECTOR ART!

It's amazing how few web designers realize how

powerful Fireworks is as an illustration tool.

Most people I know think of Fireworks as a

tool to process their finished Photoshop designs

for the web, optimizing and adding interactivity. I

have found, however, that Fireworks's vector

tools, when used in combination with stroke

and fill textures and patterns, give extraordinary

results—results that you can twist, scale, and

even export to FreeHand or Illustrator without

losing image quality.

Project 1

Unbelievable Vector Illustration

by Lisa Lopuck

GETTING STARTED

The illustration you see on this page was created completely in Fireworks using vector
tools. As you can see, not only can you build illustrations as straightforward as a laptop
computer by using basic shapes and gradient fills, you also can create complex, textured
illustrations such as the life-like jaguar. This project walks you through the process of
creating a basic vector illustration and shows you how to use the Modify menu, the
Properties Inspector, and the Layers panel to bring your drawing to life. All of the
source files needed to complete the project can be found on the accompanying
CD-ROM, along with the final illustrations for you to dissect.

BUILDING UNIQUE VECTOR SHAPES

By using the Pen and Shape tools in conjunction with the Modify menu, you can create interesting new shapes from two ordinary shapes. For example, to create a crescent moon shape, you'd overlap two circles and use the topmost circle to trim the underlying one by using Intersect found in the Modify | Combine Paths menu, leaving you with a crescent. By creating a collection of unique shapes, you can draw almost anything your heart desires. In this first section, you'll create a two-toned leaf. By repeating these steps, you can create a garden of leaves and flowers for the jaguar illustration.

1 Open the **leaves.jpg** file from the **Project 1** folder on the accompanying CD-ROM.

2 In the Layers panel, lock the **Background** layer that has the leaves on it and create a new layer. Double-click the new layer and rename it **Leaves**.

Note: The best way to create your illustrations is to find a bitmap image and trace over it in a new series of layers. For this section, use **leaves.jpg** from the **Project 1** folder on the accompanying CD-ROM.

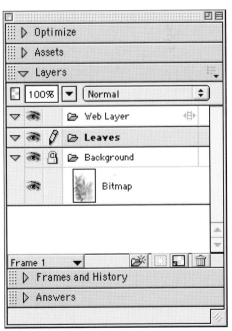

Lock the layer with the bitmap image and add a new layer named **Leaves**.

3 Select the Pen tool and click once in the document at the tip of a leaf to lay down your first point. Set your second point midway down the leaf at the fattest edge. This time, however, don't just click. In one movement, click and then drag out control handles for the point that parallels the length of the leaf. In this same manner, set your third point at the bottom tip of the leaf. Drag straight down to create handles that pull the previous path inward, resulting in an "S" curve.

Notice that as you drag, two handles extend from the point—one going up that affects the path to the previous point and one going down that affects the path to the next point.

4 To make a sharp corner, hold down the Option or Alt key and click once on the bottom point. To trace back up the leaf, click to set down your fourth point at the fattest midpoint. Drag out the handles that parallel the leaf. Click once on the original point at the top of the leaf. As you click the original point, drag a handle upward to shape the path leading off the fourth point.

You delete the lower handle extending off the bottom point to turn the sharp corner of the leaf. Note how you finish the leaf with the final step of clicking the original point at the top of leaf, dragging the handle to shape the path.

Tip: When you click to make a point, hold the mouse down and drag. This creates handles that extend out from the point that controls the curvature of the line. As you drag, watch how you drastically adjust the curvature.

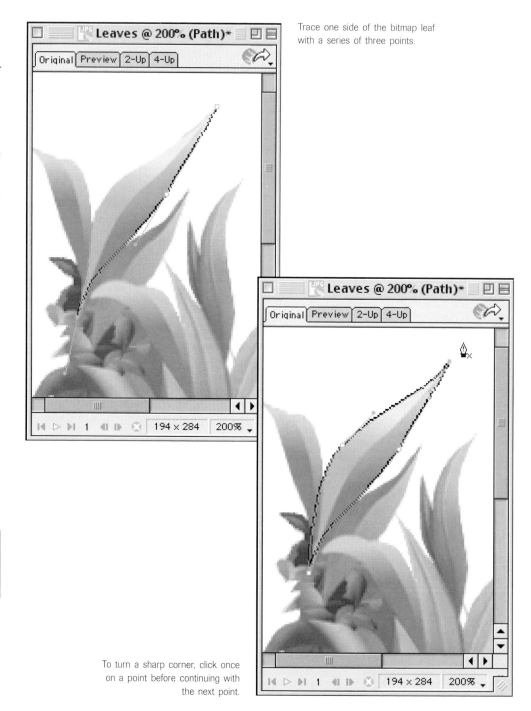

Trace one side of the bitmap leaf with a series of three points.

To turn a sharp corner, click once on a point before continuing with the next point.

5 Use the Pen tool to draw another leaf overlapping the first one. Draw the shape so that its left edge runs precisely through the middle of the first leaf and its right edge extends past the original leaf.

This shape will become the second tone of our two-tone leaf. The right edge does not need to be precise.

6 With the Pointer tool, select both shapes by holding down the Shift key. Choose Edit | Copy and then Edit | Paste. While the pasted set is selected, choose Modify | Combine Paths | Intersect.

This action creates a new shape that is the intersection of the original leaf and the second overlapping leaf. This action also deletes the original shapes, leaving you with one new shape. This is why you are working with a copied set.

7 Select and delete the remaining second shape.

You should now have just the original leaf outline and the new intersection shape. You now have the two shapes you need to create a two-toned leaf.

Draw a second, overlapping shape that runs through the midline of the original shape.

Select both shapes and choose Modify | Combine | Intersect to create a new shape.

8 Apply a different solid fill color to each shape. Repeat these steps to create a whole cluster of leaves.

> **Tip:** If you feel adventurous, you can use this same leaf-building technique to make the petals of a flower.

Repeat the steps to create multiple leaves.

ADDING TEXTURE AND COLOR

Fireworks has an amazing array of patterns and textures that produce realistic results when combined with gradient fills and various brush strokes. In this section, you'll add color and texture to the leaves you've already created or to the **leaves.png** file provided in the **Project 1** folder on the accompanying CD-ROM.

1 Open the **leaves.png** file from the **Project 1** folder on the accompanying CD-ROM or continue working with your own leaves illustration.

The leaves currently are filled with solid colors. Instead, you're going to fill each leaf with a textured gradient fill.

2 Select the dark segment of the two-toned leaf and, in the Properties Inspector, change its fill from Solid to Linear gradient. In the Properties Inspector, click on the color swatch to open the Gradient editor. In the editor, click the colored squares on either end of the gradient to adjust their colors to a medium and dark green. In the document, adjust the endpoints of the gradient handle to control its direction.

3 Select the lighter leaf segment and apply a linear gradient fill that goes from a light green to a medium green.

By changing the leaf's fill from Solid to a gradient, you add greater realism and dimension.

Apply a gradient fill to each leaf segment.

4 In the Properties Inspector, choose a texture from the Textures pop-up menu and adjust its percentage to about 30%. Uncheck the Transparent option.

Feel free to experiment with different textures for each leaf segment. Now that you have two textured gradient fills—a dark one and a light one—you can quickly apply these fills to the remaining leaf segments of the illustration. You'll do that in the next step.

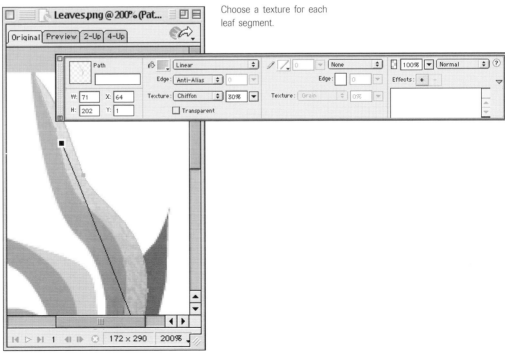

Choose a texture for each leaf segment.

5 Select and copy the leaf segment filled with the darker gradient. Shift+select all of the document's leaf segments to which you want to apply the gradient. Choose Edit | Paste Attributes. Deselect all of the segments.

You might now want to select each segment individually and adjust the fill handle to control its direction.

6 Repeat this process for the lighter gradient. Select and copy the leaf segment filled with the lighter gradient. Shift+select the segments to fill and choose Edit | Paste Attributes. Finally, adjust the fill handles as needed.

Select all of the leaf segments that will have the same fill settings and copy to clipboard.

Use the Paste Attributes command to quickly fill the remaining leaf segments.

PASTING OBJECTS INSIDE OTHER OBJECTS

It is not always possible to apply one gradient and texture to a modified shape to get the effect you desire. What you can do, however, is create a series of shapes with different fills and textures and then paste them all inside of a single shape. This is the technique used to create the three-dimensional-looking jaguar body.

1 Open **jaguar_begin.png** from the **Project 1** folder on the accompanying CD-ROM.

In this file, the head and the tail have been completed for you. Your task is to add a three-dimensional look to the cat's body. As you can see, the **Body** layer in the Layers panel contains a single outline shape of the cat's body. You will create a handful of shapes—each filled with a different color, gradient, or texture—and paste these shapes inside the body shape.

2 Turn off the **Body** layer's visibility. Create a new layer.

The layer below, the **Body Tracing** layer, contains a bitmap included as a guide for preparing your differently colored shapes. You will build them in the new layer you just created.

3 In your new layer, draw an oval shape that will be the white patch of hair on the jaguar's chest. Use the Freeform tool to mold the oval into a more organic shape.

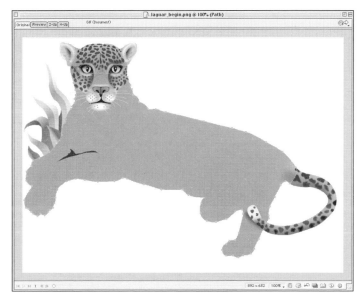

The jaguar's body is a single shape created with the Pen tool.

Modify a basic oval shape with the Reshape Area tool to create the chest patch.

4 In the Properties Inspector, adjust the shape's fill to have a 15-pixel feathered edge. Choose the Chiffon texture set at 25% with the Transparent option checked.

Apply a feathered edge and choose a transparent texture.

The patch of hair comes alive with fill effects.

5 Repeat this process until you have a series of individual shapes, each with a different fill color, texture, and feathered edge. In some cases, try filling the shape with a gradient.

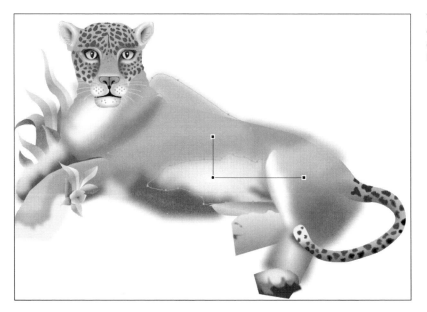

You should have a number of variously colored shapes extending beyond the body shape.

6 Select all of your shapes and select Cut. Turn on the **Body** layer's visibility, select the body shape, and choose Edit | Paste Inside. Turn on the **Spots** and **Plants1** layers' visibility.

Voilá! You now have an unbelievably realistic vector illustration.

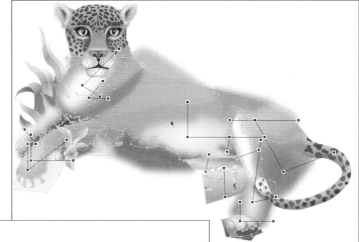

Select all of the colorized shapes and cut and paste them inside the body shape.

Layers of multiple vector objects give breadth and depth to your illustration.

Turning on the **Spots** layer completes the illustration.

MODIFICATIONS

The techniques covered in this project are just the beginning! You can extend your creative options by creating custom textures and fill patterns. You also can apply effects in the Properties Inspector to apply Photoshop filters and other effects to liven up a design. When you are through building different illustrations, such as the garden of leaves and the jaguar, you can group them and then combine them into new illustrations. You can scale and stretch each illustration to size without compromising image quality.

1   Open **lava_tile.png** from the **Project 1** folder. This file is a textured design that will tile seamlessly, meaning it will repeat across the page with no visible edges. Save the design as either a PNG, a GIF, or any other file format that Fireworks recognizes and place the file in the Configurations | Textures folder (in the Fireworks folder on your computer).

2   Quit and restart Fireworks. Create a shape and, in the Properties Inspector, choose your new custom texture from the pop-up list.

You must restart Fireworks for the program to load your new custom texture into the menus.

Note: You can also save your custom tile into the Configurations | Patterns folder on your computer. After restarting Fireworks, you can fill objects with your custom pattern by selecting it in the Properties Inspector.

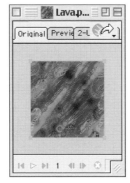

Build a seamless tile and save it in the Configurations | Textures folder.

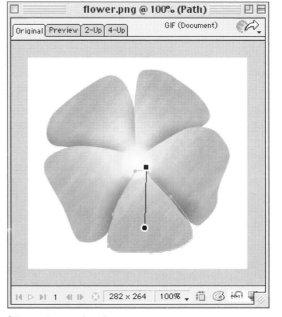

Select a shape and apply your new texture.

After restarting Fireworks, your custom texture will appear as a choice in the pop-up menu.

3 To apply a Photoshop filter to a selected object, choose Edit | Preferences. In the dialog box, choose Folders from the pop-up list. Check the Photoshop Plug-Ins option and then locate your Photoshop 5.5 Plug-Ins folder. (Photoshop 6 plug-ins do not work with Fireworks.)

4 Select an object in your document. In the Properties Inspector, click the Plus (+) sign icon and select a Photoshop filter from the pop-up menu.

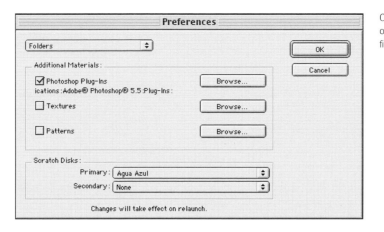

Check the Photoshop Plug-Ins option to access Photoshop filters as live effects.

5 After building an illustration out of a host of vector objects, select the objects and group them. Then combine your illustrations into a new scene like this laptop illustration.

In this example, I first combined the garden of leaves with the jaguar and grouped the result. Then I scaled the jaguar/garden group to size and pasted it inside the laptop's screen.

Note: There are two ways to scale an illustration in Fireworks. After grouping the objects of your illustration, you can simply click and drag one of the corner blue points to scale. Scaling this way, however, will throw off your gradient fills. The best way to scale is to select and group your illustration and then use the Scale tool in the Tool panel, or you can access Free Transform from the Modify | Transform menu.

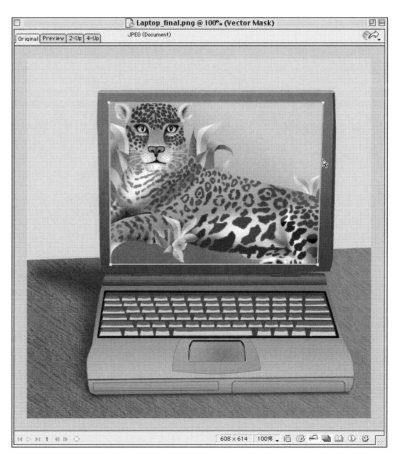

Group each element of your illustration and use the Scale tool to size each element.

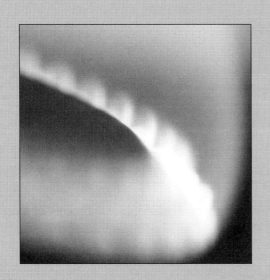

BRILLIANT BITMAP
COLLAGE

"America is a land of opportunity

and don't ever forget it."

—WILL ROGERS

BUILDING WORLD-CLASS COMPOSITIONS

Fireworks is a powerful bitmap editor, and its

capabilities far exceed that of minor bitmap

editing or using bitmap images as fills and

textures. You can design compositions as

complex as any you've seen on magazine

covers or world-class web sites. In this project,

you'll learn how to use techniques such as

Layer Blending modes, opacity, and masking,

and you'll use tools such as the Rubber

Stamp and Transform tools to build a

composite image.

Project 2

Brilliant Bitmap Collage

Joyce J. Evans

GETTING STARTED

The collage you'll produce in this project primarily consists of one image. Several smaller images have been blended into the composition by using masking techniques, rotation, and Layer Blending modes. Composite images such as this are often used in web site design for banners, logos, or backgrounds. In this project, I'll walk you through the process of altering the shape of the nautilus seashell and applying Blending modes to make a stylized background design. You also will use masks, the Rubber Stamp tool, the Scale tool, and the Properties Inspector to add effects and textures.

Note: The final illustrations and all the source files needed to complete the project can be found in the **Project 2** folder on the accompanying CD-ROM. You also will find files that have been saved after each section, so you can jump in at any time during the process.

ALTERING A BITMAP SHAPE

By using the Selection tools, copy (or cut) and paste, layers, rotation, and the Rubber Stamp tool, you can change the shape of the nautilus seashell that is the main focal point of the composition. You'll copy a portion of the shell and rotate it to the desired angle. You'll then repair the resulting seam with the Rubber Stamp tool. To finish the shell, you'll remove the black fringe around its edges.

Note: If you'd rather skip this portion of the project, you'll find a saved image of the altered shell, named **alteredshell.png**, in the **Project 2** folder on the accompanying CD-ROM. Copy the folder and images to your hard drive and move to the "Massaging Pixels" section later in this project.

1 Launch Fireworks and start a new 600×600–pixel document with a custom background color of Hex #0000FF and the default resolution of 72. Save the document as **myshell.png**.

The document is now ready for the shell; however, you will work on the shell separately and add it in later.

2 Open the **shell.gif** file from the **Project 2** folder on the accompanying CD-ROM. First you need to get rid of the background color. To do so, select the Magic Wand tool in the toolbar. In the Properties Inspector, set the Wand's edge from Hard to Anti-alias (in the drop-down menu). Click once on the background around the shell and press the Delete key.

3 Open the Optimize panel and set the Export File Format to GIF. Set the Colors amount to 256, use Index Transparency, Web Snap Adaptive, No Dither, and No Matte Color. Choose File | Export (Images Only will already be the choice), name the file **shell2.gif**, and save.

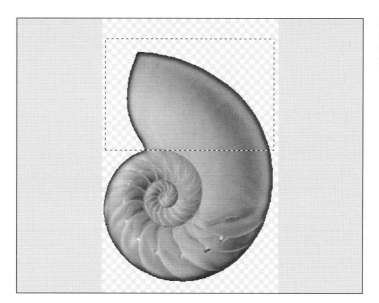

Make a selection around the top portion of the shell. You will rotate just the selected portion.

4 Select the Marquee tool (rectangle) and make a selection of the top portion of the shell that touches the center, curved area. Choose Edit | Copy, deselect, and then Edit | Paste.

By copying and pasting the selection, it becomes a separate object that you can manipulate independently.

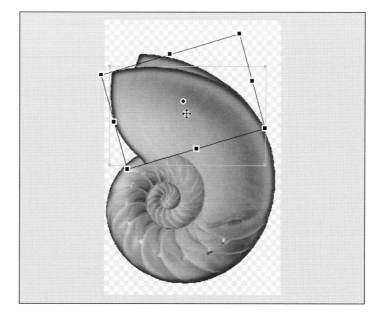

Rotate the copied portion of the shell and move it into a new position.

5 While the pasted element is selected, choose the Scale tool in the Tool panel. Rotate the image counter-clockwise about 45 degrees. Move the object to the left until the bottom edge matches the edges on the right side of the shell. Double-click to apply the transformation.

Don't worry about the bottom portion going into the curved center; you will take care of that later.

Note: To rotate a selection with the Scale tool, move your cursor to one of the corners until you see a little rounded icon. Click and drag to rotate. The figure to the right shows what it looks like prior to double-clicking to accept the transformation.

6 With the Lasso tool, select and delete the shell portion that is covering up the spiral shape.

7 Select Bitmap in Layer 1 (the top portion of the shell) and lower the opacity to 80%. Select the Polygon Lasso tool, make a selection of everything that goes below the outside edge of the main shell, and press the Delete key. Return the opacity to 100%.

By temporarily lowering the opacity, you can see through to the underlying shell.

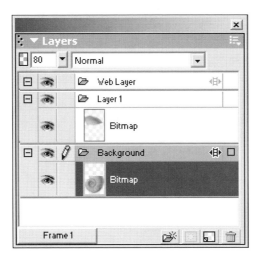

The Layers panel should contain two bitmap objects.

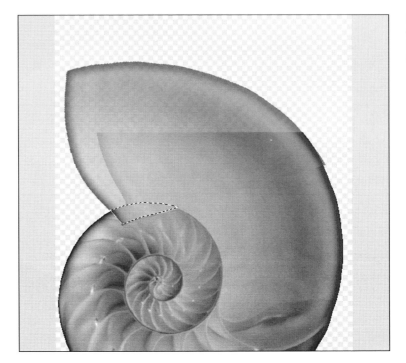

Draw a selection on the overlapped area and delete it to reveal the underlying curved shape.

8 With the top bitmap selected in the Layers panel, choose Modify | Merge Down from the menu. Double-click the Background layer and rename it **shell**.

You now have a single modified bitmap shell. Because it is a single bitmap object, it will be easier to make further repairs to it such as fixing the line that connects the top and bottom portions of the shell.

After choosing Merge Down from the menu, you'll have a single bitmap object.

MASSAGING PIXELS

Now that you have adjusted the shape of the bitmap, the next step is to massage the image itself to get rid of the hard lines produced by your changes. In this section, you'll use the Rubber Stamp tool in conjunction with the Selection tools to control your editing.

1 Zoom in so you can see the hard connecting line. Using the Polygon Lasso tool, make a selection around the line area. Choose Select | Feather from the menu and enter **10** pixels.

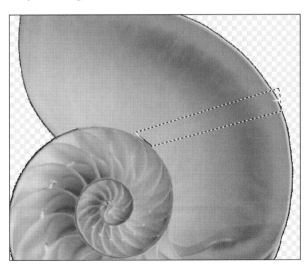

Zoom into the area where the two bitmaps connected and draw a selection around it.

2 Select the Rubber Stamp tool and, in the Properties Inspector, enter **20** for the Size. Check the Source Aligned option and lower the opacity to 70%. Position your cursor so that the crosshair is below the line you want to cover. Press and hold the Alt or Option key and click to set your source point. (When you release, you will see a blue circle around the source area.) Now, as if you were painting, draw along the line to make the repair.

By using only 70% opacity, the repair and color variations are a lot less noticeable.

> **Note:** There are two pointers, or cursors, when using the Rubber Stamp tool. The round blue circle (which is visible when you release the mouse after setting the source) is the source pointer (the area you want to copy from), and the Rubber Stamp is your actual cloning brush. By using the Source Aligned option each time you click or drag the mouse, the two pointers move together.

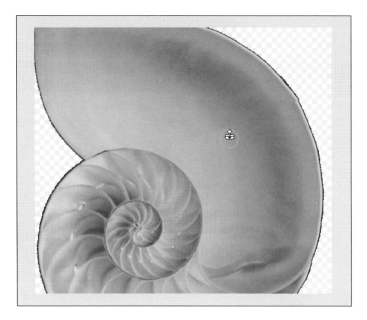

When working with the Rubber Stamp tool, you'll see two cursors moving around—the source point and the cloning point.

> **Tip:** You can use the Rubber Stamp tool without making a selection. We used a feathered selection in this case because we wanted to clone within a specific area and yet not produce harsh lines when cloning at the edges of our selection. You should also try changing the cloning source point a few times to make the cloning look less obvious.

REMOVING THE FRINGE AROUND A BITMAP

When working with bitmap graphics, the image often has been composited to a white or colored background. Even after using the Magic Wand tool to remove the background color, you'll see a "halo" around the image. This thin halo is what blends the image gently into the background color so that it doesn't have jagged edges. If you plan to put the image on top of another color, however, you must get rid of the halo; otherwise, your image will have a mismatched fringe. This project shows you how to remove the fringe.

1 To remove the black edge of the image, select the Magic Wand tool. In the Properties Inspector, set the wand's Tolerance to **0** and select the Anti-Aliased option from the pull-down menu.

2 Click once in the transparent area around the image to select it. To remove the fringe, you'll need to add at least 2 pixels to your selection by choosing Select | Expand Marquee. In the dialog box that opens, enter **2** pixels and click OK. Press the Delete key to remove the fringed edge.

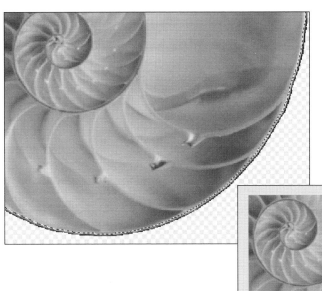

An expanded selection ensures that the entire fringe will be deleted.

The black "halo" has been removed from the outside edge of the shell.

3 Select and copy the shell bitmap. Open the **myshell.png** file that you made in the first section and paste the shell into the file. A dialog box will appear, asking how you'd like to paste the image. Choose Don't Resample. Double-click Layer 1 in the Layers panel and rename it **Shell**. Save the document as **workingshell1.png**.

You'll notice that the shell blends nicely into the blue background because you removed the black fringing.

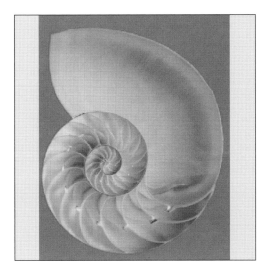

The shell on its new background.

ADDING AN INTERESTING BACKGROUND

In Fireworks, you can produce an interesting background by using the various Layer Blending modes or by using textures and patterns. In this section, you'll produce a unique backdrop for the nautilus shell by building a background from pieces of the shell and then modifying those pieces with Layer Blending modes and textures.

1 Open the **workingshell1.png** file from the **Project 2** folder on the accompanying CD-ROM or continue working with your own file. Add a new layer on top of the **Shell** layer. Double-click the new layer and name it **Shellbackground**.

2 With the Marquee tool, draw a selection over the bottom portion of the shell, just below the center curved part. Copy and paste the selected portion into the **Shellbackground** layer.

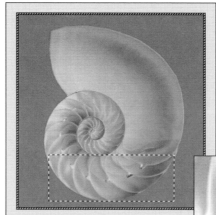

Copy the bottom portion of the shell and paste it into a new layer.

3 Paste one more time. Choose Modify | Transform | Flip Horizontal from the menu. Move the flipped version to the top of the canvas and the bottom version to the bottom of the canvas. By pulling on the objects' handles, stretch each piece to fill one half of the document. By stretching the images, you make an abstracted design for your collage.

Stretch the two shell portions to fit the background area.

4 Select the top bitmap in the **Shellbackground** layer. Choose Modify | Merge Down.

By merging down, you combine the two halves into one bitmap image.

5 To add effects to the image, click the Plus (+) sign icon to access the Effects list in the Properties Inspector. Select Adjust Color | Curves and click the Auto button.

Tip: You can also make each portion of the shell the same shape by entering height and width values of **850** (Width) and **470** (Height) into the Info panel and then pressing the Enter or Return key.

6 Click the Plus (+) sign icon again to add another effect. This time choose Adjust Color | Color Fill. Use a red fill, Hex # FF0000. Change the Blending mode to Saturation.

7 Click the Plus (+) sign icon to add a third effect. Choose Adjust Color | Color Fill. Use a red fill again, Hex # FF0000. Change the Blending mode to Difference.

8 To compound the composition's effects, change the Shellbackground's Layer Blending mode from Normal to Lighten in the pull-down menu on the Layers panel.

The layer's Blending mode interacts with the colors of the layers below as well as the blue canvas color. Experiment with the canvas color for a different look (choose Modify | Canvas | Canvas Color).

9 In the Layers panel, add a new layer and drag it below the other two layers. On this new **Layer 1**, use the Rectangle tool to draw four separate rectangle shapes over the background area. In the Properties Inspector, fill each rectangle with the following settings. (You can click on the Fill color swatch to access the full range of fill options.)

Top left: Fill color #66FF99 (light green), Edge: Feather of 50, Texture: Line–Horiz 3 at 70%, Normal blending mode.

Top right: Fill color #0066FF (bright blue), Edge: Feather of 50, no Texture, Normal blending mode.

Bottom left: Fill color #0066FF (bright blue), Edge: Feather of 50, Texture: Onyx at 20%, Multiply Blending mode. (Blending mode can be changed in the Layers panel or the Properties Inspector.)

Bottom right: Fill color #FF6633 (orange), Edge: Feather of 50, Texture: Scratch at 40%, Screen blending mode.

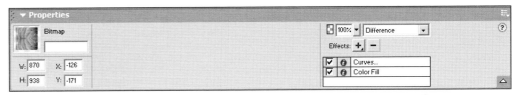

You can significantly alter the look of a bitmap by applying a series of effects.

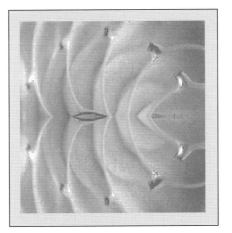

Layer Blending modes affect the color interaction between an object and its the underlying objects.

Note: Blending modes are based on calculations that Fireworks makes on values, which are associated with pixels. The values used in the calculations depend on the Blending mode chosen and could include hue, RGB values, brightness, or the transparency of the pixels.

Note that you don't have to draw precise quarters for this exercise. In fact, it's better if you don't draw precise shapes. Adding the rectangles introduces texture and depth.

10 Select the **Shell** layer and lower its opacity to 70%.

11 To finish the background, open the **starfish.png** file from the **Project 2** folder on the accompanying CD-ROM. Select the **Shellbackground** layer and add a new layer. Name this layer **Starfish**. Copy the **starfish.png** image and paste it into the **Starfish** layer. Select Don't Resample when the choice appears.

You are adding the **Starfish** layer above the **Shellbackground** layer so that it doesn't affect any of the Blending mode effects you've already achieved.

The shell combined with four rectangles adds texture and depth to the composition.

12 Drag the corners of the starfish image to fit the document.

You can stretch and resize the image to achieve a desirable location. Lower the opacity of this layer to 30%.

Add the **starfish.png** file to complete the composition.

ADDING IMAGES INSIDE THE SHELL

In this section, you'll add to your composition by pasting objects inside of other objects. When you paste one image inside of another, you make a mask group.

1 Open the **coral.png** file from the **Project 2** folder on the accompanying CD-ROM. Copy the coral image and paste it into the **Shell** layer of your composition. Drag the coral image to the top area of the shell.

2 Draw a rectangle over the coral image and fill with a Radial gradient. Shift+select both the coral image and the rectangle. Choose Modify | Mask | Group as Mask.

The Radial gradient fades out the edges and leaves the center portion visible. It also adds a bit of light to the center of the coral.

3 In the Properties Inspector, click the Fill color swatch to access the gradient settings. Click on the transparent gradient slider and change the opacity to 70%.

4 Open **hermit.png** from the **Project 2** folder on the accompanying CD-ROM. Using the Marquee tool, draw a rectangle around the hermit crab. Copy the hermit crab and paste it into a new layer of your composition, just above the **Shell** layer. Name the new layer **Hermit**. When you paste, choose Don't Resample. Resize the crab to a Width of **300** and a Height of **250**. (Make these changes in the Properties Inspector.)

5 Select the Rectangle tool and, in the Properties Inspector, change the Edge option to a Feather of 50. Draw a rectangle over the crab. It will automatically fill with the radial gradient you last used. Change the gradient to Starburst. Select the gradient fill and the crab and choose Modify | Mask | Group as Mask.

You might wonder why I added the feather to the rectangle prior to grouping it as a mask. I found that if I did not feather first, the image's edge was visible after masking, and moving the gradient handles didn't remove the edge. By applying a feathered edge on the rectangle first, I could remove the edges.

Note: You can change the position of any gradient by dragging and moving the gradient handles. If the handles are not visible, click the Mask thumbnail in the Layers panel and then click the Pen icon.

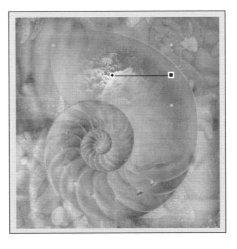

When grouped with a radial gradient, the coral image fades at the edges and brightens in the center.

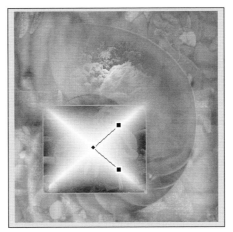

Prepare a feathered rectangle filled with a Starburst gradient to use as a mask for the crab.

6 In the Layers panel, click on the crab's mask thumbnail. Click the Pen icon to edit the mask. Adjust the gradient to reveal just the portion of the crab you want. Move the crab to the center of the shell and resize it to fit.

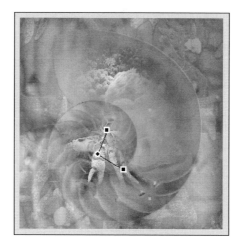

Adjust the gradient with the gradient handles to reveal different parts of the crab.

MODIFICATIONS

Using the bitmap editing techniques discussed throughout this project, the innovative possibilities are truly endless. You might now be asking, however, what can you do with such a great collage? This final section will discuss different uses for collages in a web site.

1 Open **workingshell3.png** from the **Project 2** folder or continue working with your composition. Select the shell graphic in the **Shellbackground** layer. In the Properties Inspector, click the Add Effect button and select one of the effects in the list.

In this example, I applied Alien Skin's Swirl filter. Fireworks allows you to use filters from other companies, including Adobe Photoshop filters.

> **Note:** You can download Alien Skin's Eye Candy 4000 pack for free from the web (**www.alienskin.com/ ec4k/ec4000_main.html**). If you don't want to get or use this, I saved a copy named **shellbitmap.png** that can be used later in this section.

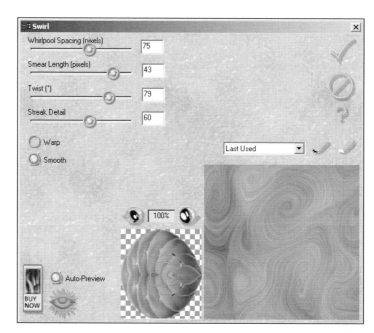

You can use third-party filters such as Alien Skin's Swirl filter from the Eye Candy 3 collection.

2 Choose Modify | Canvas | Canvas Size and change both the Height and Width to **800**.

Your composition is now suitable to use as a background image for either a web site or a Flash movie.

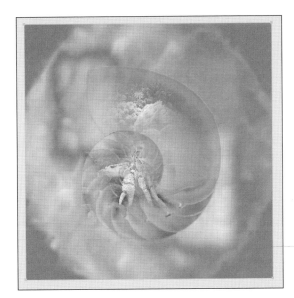

By increasing the canvas size, you can prepare your composition for use as an HTML page background tile.

3 To design a web banner, hide **Layer 1** (with the rectangles) and the **Starfish** layer. Shift+select all remaining objects: the shell, coral, and hermit. Group these objects (Ctrl+G/Cmd+G) and move them to the upper-left side of the document.

4 You can reposition the shell to a more pleasing location by selecting the three grouped objects, choosing Modify | Free Transform, and rotating them.

If you rotate the shell totally upside down as I did, you will have another problem—the crab is now upside down.

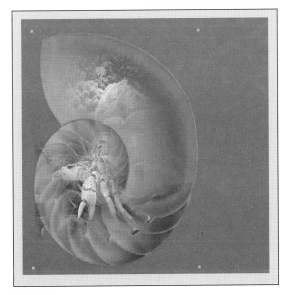

Group a few of the elements to build a web page banner.

5 Select the three grouped objects and choose Modify | Ungroup (Shift+Ctrl+G/Shift+Cmd+G). Now you can select and rotate just the crab. Shift+select the three objects again and regroup them.

Note: You can access the Rotate function by selecting any of the Transform tools in the Tools panel.

The crab has been rotated and moved.

6 In the Layers panel, all that should be visible is the Group: 3 objects and the **Shellbackground**. In the Optimize panel, choose JPEG at 80% Quality and export.

A copy named **shellbitmap.jpg** is saved in the **Project 2** folder. The reason you exported is that you need a flattened bitmap image to use in the masthead. If you had merged the layers and objects, you would have changed the color of the image to gold because of the Blending modes used.

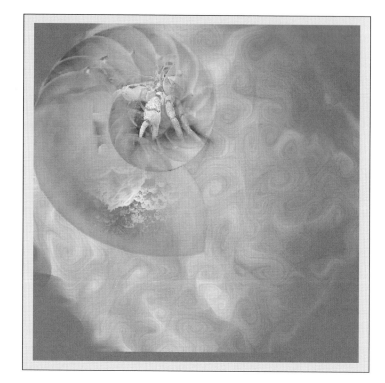

The composition after being converted to a bitmap.

7 With the Rounded Rectangle tool (the default Rectangle Roundness of 30 is fine), draw a large rectangle across the top of the document, about 600×100 pixels. Fill with any color, and use no stroke. Draw a second rectangle that is 100×600. Line them up together to form an inverted L.

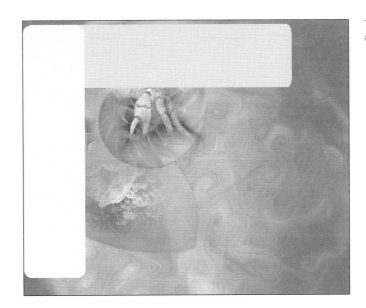

The rectangles drawn for a masthead shape.

8 Shift+select both rectangles and choose Modify | Combine Paths | Union. You now have one shape. To make the inside corner into a curve, draw another rounded rectangle with a size of about 609×560. Position it to cover the square angle.

The rectangle is so large because the rounded outside and bottom corners need to clear the straight edges of the top and side bars so that a curve isn't added in those areas.

A rounded rectangle added to make a curved corner.

9 Shift+select the L shape and the rounded rectangle. Choose Modify | Combine Paths | Punch.

You now have an inverted L shape with a rounded inside corner.

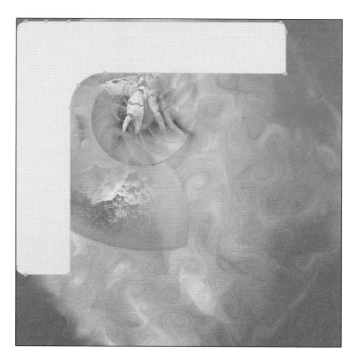

A vector shape with a rounded inside corner that will be used for a masthead.

10 To place the composition into the vector shape, choose Edit | Cut. Select the vector shape and choose Edit | Paste Inside. Notice the little cloverleaf in the center of the document. Click and drag it to position the image inside the vector shape.

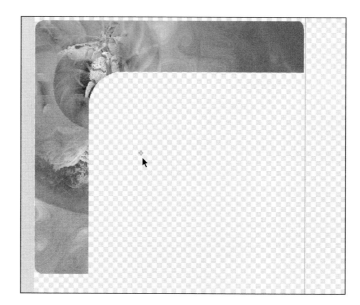

The cloverleaf icon you drag to position the image within the vector shape.

11 Add some text and a drop shadow. Now you have
a masthead.

The finished masthead.

EXPORTING EXCELLENCE

"Virtue results from habit... For we learn a craft by producing the same product that we produce when we have learned it, becoming builders, e.g., by building and harpists by playing the harp... Virtue requires habituation, and therefore requires practice, not just theory."

—ARISTOTLE

OPTIMAL PERFORMANCE FROM WEB PAGE DESIGNS

Picture this. You have just used Fireworks to

create a design masterpiece with an animated,

interactive intricacy that belies its simplicity.

Enchanted, you set aside your chisel and...uh-oh.

How are you going to export this thing out of

Fireworks, optimized for the web so that it down-

loads for the user in 20 seconds or less and is

easy to maintain? In this project, you'll learn

strategies for slicing, optimizing, and exporting

your designs for optimal web performance.

Project 3

Exporting Excellence

by Jeffrey Bardzell

GETTING STARTED

In this project, you will optimize and export a complex page design. You will slice and optimize different sections of the image as GIFs and JPEGs, and you will use related features like selective JPEG compression along the way.

The web page for this project contains both animation and interactivity, which is going to foil any simple slicing scheme. The icons in the lower-right corner are simple rollovers that also activate a disjoint rollover. The byline underneath the title is actually part of an animation of scrolling text.

Thus, you will have to use slicing for three unrelated purposes: image optimization, animation, and interactivity. In addition, you will use slicing to maximize your productivity as you transition from Fireworks to an HTML editor. Understanding these different purposes of slicing is the key to successfully exporting—and later maintaining—sophisticated page designs.

OUTLINING THE CHALLENGES

The web page design in this project was purposefully designed so that it would be difficult to export. The design presents two areas of difficulty that will be addressed:

- The page contains a mix of photographic and drawn images; each exports better as a different file type.
- The design has a mix of animation and interactivity.

The first step to successfully optimizing and exporting any design is understanding its structure so that you can best determine how to prepare it for export. This first section will pick apart the **elearning_times_start.png** file found in the **Project 3** folder on the accompanying CD-ROM.

1 Open the **elearning_times_start.png** file included in the **Project 3** folder on the accompanying CD-ROM.

Notice that the left side of the image is static, meaning there is no animation or interactivity. The challenge will be finding the best optimization solution. The right side of the image has a couple things going on. First, just under the title is a byline that says, "A newsletter for faculty and instructors." In fact, the byline is the first frame of an animation.

2 Open the Frames panel (choose Window | Frames) and click Frame 2 and then Frame 3 to see the byline's animation. Click back on Frame 1.

This animation will work quite well as an animated GIF because it contains only text and graphics, not photographs.

3 Click Frame 2.

The buttons along the bottom of the design will be rollover buttons. The photographs you see on Frame 2 are the button's *over states*—what the button looks like when the user rolls over them. Their normal, undisturbed states appear on Frame 1.

Note: The figures in this project are provided courtesy of Photodisc.

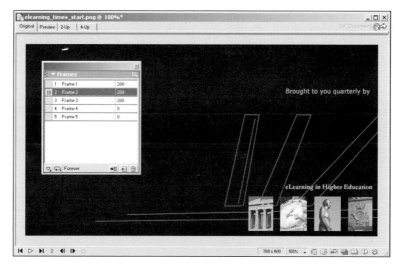

Frame 2 shows the second frame of the animation, the over states of the buttons, and one of the states of the disjoint rollover.

4 Click Frame 3, 4, and then 5.

On each frame, you'll see a different set of instructions just above the buttons. When the user rolls over each of the buttons, the appropriate text instructions will appear to provide an explanation of the button.

> **Note:** When one graphic causes another graphic to change elsewhere on the page, it is called a *disjoint rollover* (sometimes called a *swap* or *remote rollover*).

> **Note:** As you can see, Frame 2 has three different uses. It contains the second frame of the byline animation, the over states of all four buttons, and the explanation of one of the buttons. How does Fireworks know to export one as a simple animation, another as a rollover, and the third as a disjoint rollover? The answer, of course, is slicing.

Frame 3 contains only content for the animation and the disjoint rollover. There is no information for the button rollovers because they use only the first two frames.

SLICING A NESTED TABLE STRUCTURE

HTML tables have the potential to get extremely complex. The best way to keep the page simple is to build a nested table structure in which one simplified "super" table holds a number of other tables in place. In this section, you'll slice the design to create a super table of just four cells. In the next section, you'll export the smaller tables that will nest inside each of the four cells. A nested table structure results in a page that is much easier to maintain than a single-table page made up of 300 cells.

1 Continue working with the **elearning_times_start.png** file included on the accompanying CD in the **Project 3** folder. Choose File | Save As to rename and save the file as **elearning_times_supertable.png**.

2 If the ruler is not visible, choose View | Ruler. From the left-edge ruler, drag out a guide so that it is to the left of the Latin text. Double-click the guide and enter **420** pixels.

3 From the top ruler, drag down three more guides. Double-click the three new guides to enter the following positions:

89 pixels

110 pixels

285 pixels

If you don't add this guide now, you won't have anywhere to put the animation slice at the end of the project.

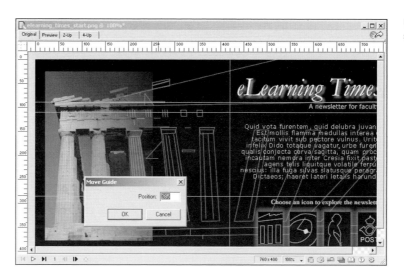

Use guides to plan out a simplified slicing structure.

4 Select the Slice tool and draw slices over five regions. Draw one slice to cover the whole left half. Draw another to cover the title area to the right. Draw a third in the narrow region over the animated GIF byline. Create a fourth slice over the right text portion and a fifth to cover the space for the buttons and instruction line.

By drawing slices, you are actually creating an HTML table structure. Fireworks will output the table structure in an HTML file that can be edited or used as is with Dreamweaver. Each sliced area will become a separate graphic. Each separate graphic can have its own optimization setting.

5 Choose File | Export.

At this point in the project, you should not be worried about optimization or behaviors. You are just creating a custom table for an HTML editor like Dreamweaver.

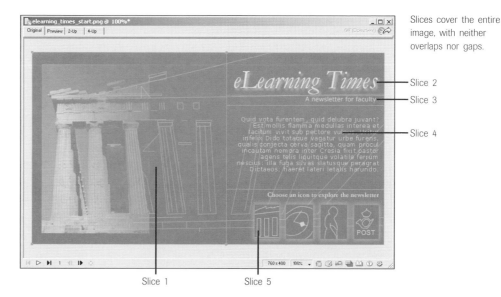

Slices cover the entire image, with neither overlaps nor gaps.

Slice 2

Slice 3

Slice 4

Slice 1   Slice 5

6 Create a new folder to which to export your design. Choose HTML and Images from the Save As Type options and check the Put Images in Subfolder option.

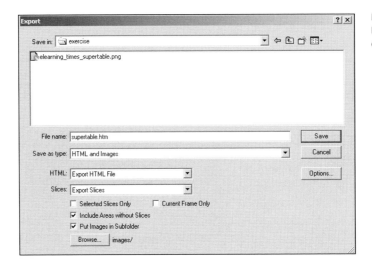

Making the right choices in the Export dialog box is critical to exporting interactive Fireworks files.

7 Click the Options button to open the HTML Setup dialog box. Click the Table tab. Select Single Table—No Spacers from the Space With options.

By choosing this option, you are telling Fireworks to generate a simple, single table structure with no tables embedded or nested within another.

8 Name your file **supertable.htm** and click Save.

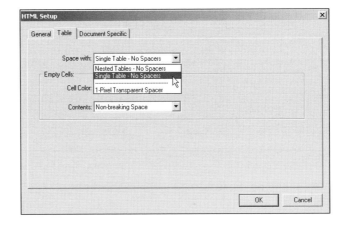

Use the Table tab to determine whether you want nested or simple tables.

OPTIMIZING AND EXPORTING THE GRAPHICS

In this section, you will optimize the graphics of the file and export them as their own table structure. Optimizing the graphics requires a new slicing strategy, so you will delete the slices made earlier and draw new slices over just the graphics. Leave the guides in place. The previous HTML table you exported is based on them, and you'll use them to draw your next set of slices.

1 Choose File | Save As and rename your file **elearning_times_imagesoptimized.png**.

2 Select and delete each of the slices created earlier. Create three new slices over the left region: one covering the leftmost photo, one covering the right graphical portion, and one covering the middle section.

Make sure the three slices fit exactly over the same area as occupied by the previous large slice.

3 Select the left and middle slices and, in the Optimize panel, choose JPEG set to 65% quality. Select the right slice and choose GIF, Adaptive palette, 32 colors.

Because the left slice covers a photograph, 65% JPEG does a great job at compressing the image. The right slice contains purely graphic content that does well as a GIF with only 32 colors. Because the middle slice covers an area with both photographs and graphics, neither the JPEG nor the GIF format works entirely well. For such a situation, Fireworks offers selective JPEG compression that enables you to compress a selected region of a slice with a different JPEG setting.

4 Turn off the slice overlay by pressing the left Hide/Show Slices button in the Tools panel. With the Lasso tool, draw a selection around the line drawing portions of the image. Choose Modify | Selective JPEG | Save Selection as JPEG Mask.

5 Click the red Exit Bitmap Mode button to return to regular vector mode.

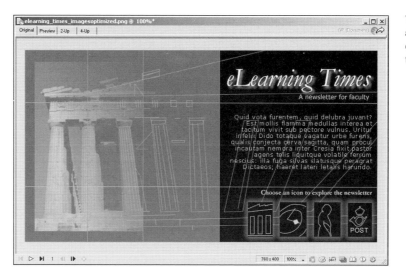

These three slices are used for image optimization rather than table creation.

Tip: To preview the effects of your optimization settings, click the Preview tab at the top of the document. Click the Original tab to continue working.

Exit Bitmap Mode

You can make a selective JPEG mask from any selection.

6 Turn on the Slice view and select the middle slice. In the Optimize panel, click the Pencil icon next to the Selective Quality option. In the dialog box that opens, check the Enable Selective Quality option and enter **80**. Click OK.

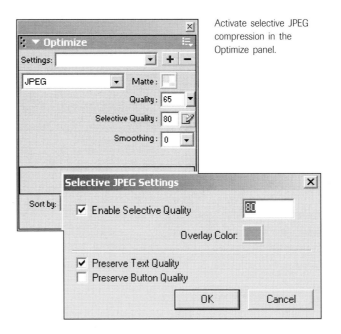

Activate selective JPEG compression in the Optimize panel.

7 Shift+select all three slices that you optimized. Choose File | Export. In the Export dialog box, choose HTML and Images from the Save As Type options. Choose Export Slices from the Slices options. Check the Selected Slices Only and Put Images in Subfolder options. Uncheck the Include Areas Without Slices option. Name the file **three_slices.htm** and click Save.

These settings will export only your three sliced areas, not the entire design. After exporting, you'll use Dreamweaver to embed the **three_slices.htm** into the **supertable.htm** file.

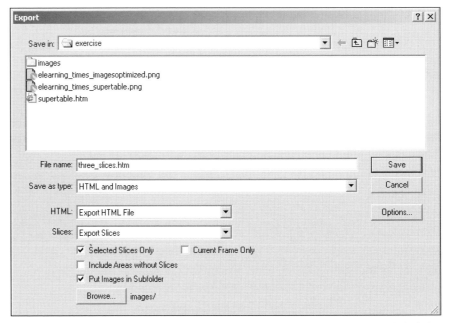

Choose Selected Slices Only to make sure you export only these three slices rather than the whole design.

8 Launch Dreamweaver and open the **supertable.htm** file you exported earlier in the project. Click the large graphic in the left cell and delete it.

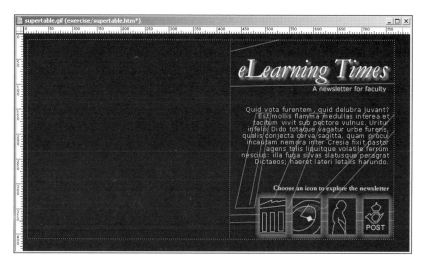

You can delete the large graphic in Dreamweaver; it was just a placeholder.

> **Note:** When you work in Dreamweaver, you normally should define a new site using the Site menu. By defining a site, you tell Dreamweaver what folder on your computer will mirror the folder structure on the server. For this project, however, it is not necessary to define a site.

9 In the Object panel, click the Insert Fireworks HTML icon. Browse to your **three_slices.htm** file and click OK. Choose File | Save.

Your three slices, which are really a three-cell table structure, will fit neatly inside the empty cell.

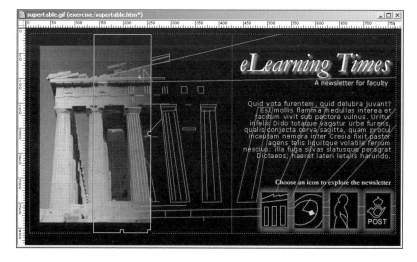

The page looks pretty much the same, but the graphics look better and take less time to download.

OPTIMIZING THE NAVIGATION BAR

By using nested tables, you ensure that your tables each have only one function: The super table provides the overall layout, and each nested table within contains a graphical or interactive element. In this section, you'll optimize and export the navigation bar in the lower-right cell and the title and animation in the upper-right cell. The assets for the navigation bar and animation have already been prepared for you in the **elearning_times_nav.png** file. After you export these regions, you'll use Dreamweaver to embed them in your super table.

1 Open the **elearning_times_nav.png** file provided in the **Project 3** folder on the accompanying CD-ROM.

Optimizing slices when multiple frames are involved can be tricky because slices are shared across frames. You cannot, for example, optimize the slice over the icons in Frame 1 as GIFs and then optimize the slice over the photographs in Frame 2 as JPEGs. The only thing you can do is find the best optimization for both of them.

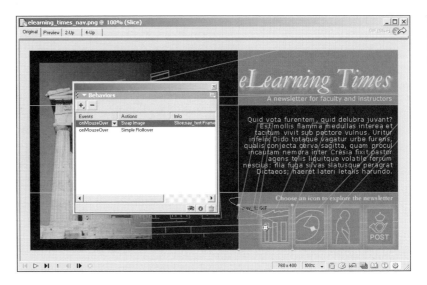

The slices and disjoint rollovers have been added in this version to save you a couple of steps.

2 Select the slice covering the disjoint rollover text and click the 2-Up tab at the top of the dialog box. Choose GIF (Slice, f1) from the drop-down menu below the lower-left corner of the image. This toggles the left page from original to optimization preview. Use the Hand tool to center the slice in the Preview window.

This slice will be easy to optimize because it contains only text. With so few colors, you know in advance that the slice will make a nice GIF.

3 Click the left preview pane to select it. In the Optimize panel's Settings drop-down menu, choose the GIF Adaptive 256 setting.

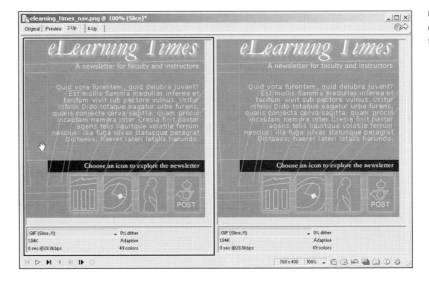

Use the Hand tool to center the image in the Preview window.

4 Click the right preview pane and, in the Optimize panel, choose the GIF Adaptive setting. Change the colors to 8 by selecting 8 from the Colors drop-down menu.

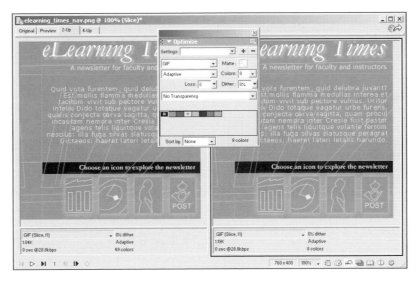

Use the 2-Up Preview mode to compare the range of GIF quality settings and sizes.

5 Now optimize the first navigation bar, or nav bar, icon. Still in 2-Up Preview mode, click the slice that contains the word "POST" (the last icon). That slice becomes highlighted, and the rest are grayed out. Set the left pane to GIF, Adaptive, 256 colors. Set the right pane to JPEG—Better Quality (80%).

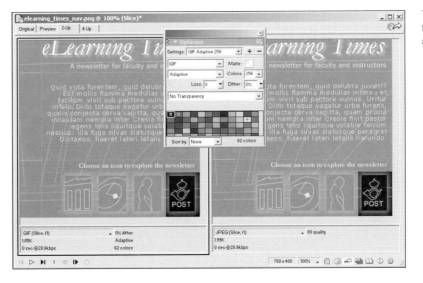

The GIF setting makes the image smaller and a bit clearer.

6 Based on the comparison, it looks like GIF is the way to go—but what about the second frame? In the lower-left corner of the document window are some VCR-like controls. The second-to-last control (on the right) is the Next Frame icon. Click it. Now the photos appear.

With the photos now in view, compare the file sizes and image quality of the two panes. The GIF is more than twice the size of the JPEG. When you multiply that increase across the four navigation bar slices, there's an additional 8KB. Therefore, the best balance of image quality and file size is the JPEG.

7 Set each of the remaining nav bar slices to JPEG 80%. Click on the Original tab to return to the main document view and save your file.

8 Shift+select all five of the nav slices and choose File | Export. In the Export dialog box, choose HTML and Images, check the Selected Slices Only and Put Images in Subfolder options, name the file **navbar.htm**, and click Save. (Be sure to save the file into the same site folder as before.)

9 In Dreamweaver, delete the placeholder graphic for the nav bar and click on the Insert Fireworks HTML icon in the Object panel. Browse to the **navbar.htm** file you just exported and click OK. To test out your page in a browser, press F12.

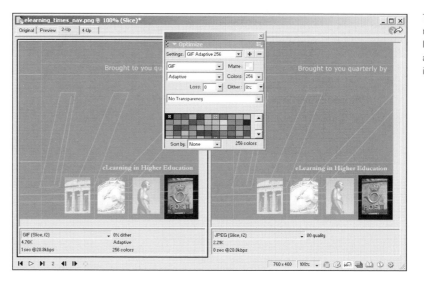

The GIF optimization setting makes the photographs too large in terms of file size and does not yield good image quality.

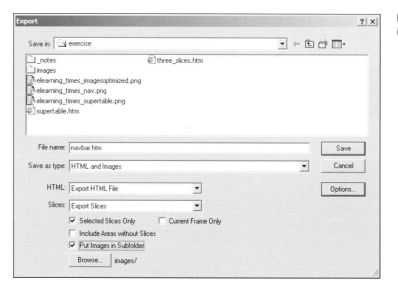

Export the navigation bar as its own sliced table structure.

Optimizing and Exporting the Animation

In this final section, you will optimize and export an animation that you can incorporate into your master Dreamweaver design along with the nav bar and optimized images. The process is similar. First you'll apply an optimization setting to a slice that covers an animation. You'll then export the selected slice but as an image only with no HTML. Finally, in Dreamweaver, you'll replace the static placeholder graphic with the new animation.

1 Open **elearning_times_nav.png** from the **Project 3** folder on the accompanying CD-ROM and save it as **elearning_times_animation.png**.

2 Select the animation slice. In the Optimize panel, choose Animated GIF, Adaptive, and 128.

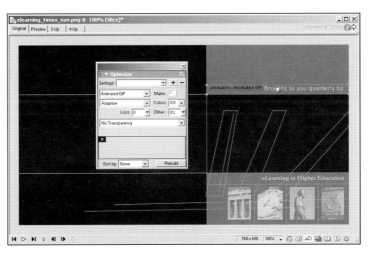

Select the slice that contains the animation and choose the Animated GIF format in the Optimize panel.

3 Cmd+click (Mac) or right-click (PC) the slice and choose Export Selected Slice from the context menu. In the Export dialog box, keep all settings but uncheck the Current Frame Only option. Name the file **animation.gif** and click Save. Be sure to save it into the **Images** folder within your **Site** folder.

Because this is just an animated GIF, you won't need any HTML or nested tables.

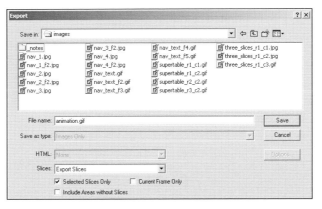

Because you have designated this as an animated slice, Fireworks correctly sets up to export.

4 In Dreamweaver, delete the placeholder graphic for the animation and insert the animated GIF in its place. To do so, you can simply double-click on the placeholder. In the Open File dialog box that appears, navigate to the **animation.gif** file and click OK.

MODIFICATIONS

In this project, you used slicing to accomplish three unrelated tasks: productivity (building the super table), optimization (the blended image), and interactivity/animation (the nav bar and animation). One issue remains: The Latin body text shouldn't be exported as a graphic but as HTML text. In this section, you will re-export the slice as a text slice as opposed to an image slice. You also will export an image to use as a background tile for the text.

1 Open **elearning_times_nav.png** and save it as **elearning_times_latin.png**. Select the Latin text object and then select the Text tool in the Tool panel. Select and copy the text. Now that the content is in the Clipboard, select and delete the text object.

2 Switch to Dreamweaver, select and delete the placeholder graphic for the text, and paste in the copied text. Select and format the text as desired using the Properties Inspector.

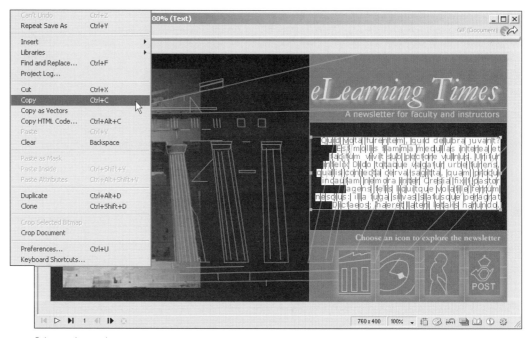

Select and copy the text.

3 Notice that the background graphic is now gone. Return to Fireworks. Click and hold on the Crop tool to reveal the whole group. From the pop-up menu of tools, select the Export Area tool. (It looks like a camera.)

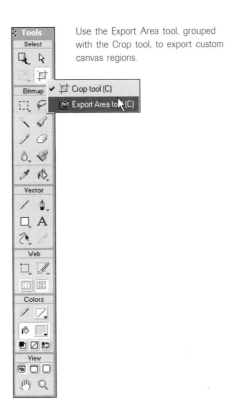

Use the Export Area tool, grouped with the Crop tool, to export custom canvas regions.

4 Draw a rectangle over the region that used to contain the Latin text. Use the existing slices as your guide. Press the Return or Enter key (or double-click the region) to open the Export Preview dialog box.

5 In the Export Preview window, use the Hand tool to center the region (hidden off to the right) into the Preview window. Set the file to export as GIF, Adaptive, 32 colors and click the Export button.

Note: If you get a warning pop-up about slices not working, just click OK and disregard it.

Use the export area to demarcate the Latin region for special export.

6 In the Export dialog box, choose Images Only from the Save As Type drop-down menu. Name the file **text_background.gif** and save it into your **Images** folder.

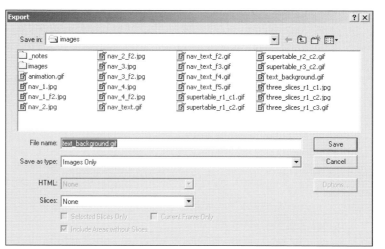

Because you are exporting a static background image, choose Images Only from the Save As Type options.

7 Return to Dreamweaver. Click anywhere in the table cell with the Latin text. This action selects the table cell so that you can apply various settings to it. In the Properties Inspector, click the folder icon to the right of the Bg text field. In the Open File dialog box, navigate to the **text_background.gif** file you just exported and click OK.

Dreamweaver inserts the graphic as the table cell's background, and the text above it remains editable.

Note: If the cell resizes, messing up the display, set the cell's height to **175** pixels and the width to **327** pixels in the Properties Inspector. This forces it to size correctly.

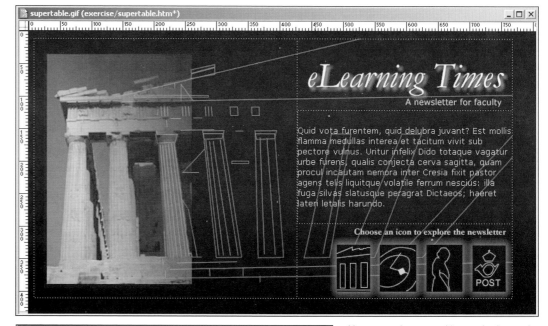

You can apply any graphic as a background tile for a table cell. Each cell can have a unique background.

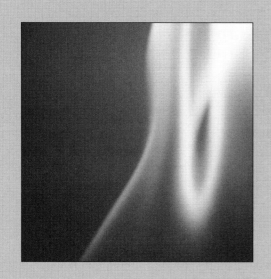

BACKGROUND
TILE DESIGN

"The power of imagination

makes us infinite."

—JOHN MUIR

CREATING AND PREVIEWING CUSTOM, SEAMLESS BACKGROUND TILES

A lot of web sites use custom background tiles

(such as the **lava_tile.png** file used at the

end of Project 1, "Unbelievable Vector

Illustration") to add depth and visual interest to

the page. Tiles can be as small as the more

familiar 100×100-pixel seamless patterns that

repeat across the page or as large as the

1,500×1,500-pixel tiles that extend beyond the

page's design so that users do not see them

repeat. Whatever tile strategy you choose,

Fireworks gives you the capability to build

such custom tiles and to use them during the

creative process to help you envision the final

page design.

Project 4

Background Tile Design

by Lisa Lopuck

GETTING STARTED

To build a custom seamless tile, you do not need anything but your imagination. You will use the standard Fireworks vector and bitmap tools to create a design and then simply save it in whatever format you like. Once saved, you'll place the tile in a special folder so that Fireworks can find it and use it as a tiled pattern to fill other objects.

> **Note:** All of the files you need for this project are included in the **Project 4** folder on the accompanying CD-ROM, along with the sample files.

CREATING A SEAMLESS PATTERN TILE

In this first section, you'll create a seamless, repeating pattern tile that will serve as the background for a web page layout. After you create your tile, you'll optimize it to reduce its file size so that it is ready for use on the web. You'll also save it into the Fireworks Configurations folder so that you can use it to simulate tiled web page designs.

1 Open the **mini_tile.png** file provided in the
     Project 4 folder on the accompanying CD-ROM.
     This file contains a grape illustration that you will
     modify to add a seamless background texture.

2 Select the Brush tool and, in the Properties Inspector, choose Air Brush (Basic) 60-pixel diameter and a light cream color. In the **Parchment** layer, spray a few patches to create a sort of parchment paper look.

3 Enlarge the canvas size by choosing Modify | Canvas | Canvas Size. Enter **300×300** for the new canvas dimensions and keep the anchor point in the center. Click OK.

To make a seamless tile, you need a larger canvas. You'll place a copy of the parchment bitmap to the side of and on top of the original so that you can smooth out the seams.

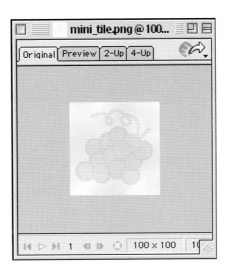

Use the Brush tool to add a parchment-like texture.

4 Select the parchment bitmap with the Pointer tool. Turn on the guides by choosing View | Rulers. Drag four guides out from the rulers and place them at all four edges of the selected bitmap.

The guides will help you position the parchment copies you'll make in the next step.

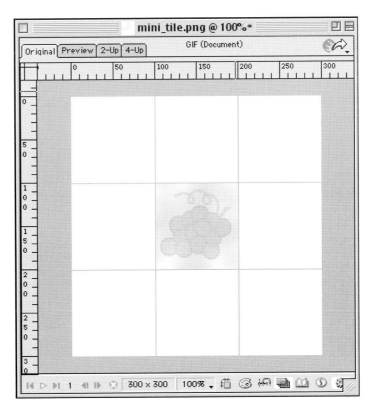

Enlarge the canvas and add guides to the edges of the parchment bitmap.

5 Hold down the Alt or Option key along with the Shift key and drag a copy of the parchment bitmap up to sit along the top edge of the original. Drag another copy off to the left edge. Shift+select all three bitmap objects and choose Modify | Flatten Selection.

Selecting the Flatten Selection action merges all three bitmaps into one. Now it is a matter of smoothing out the obvious seams where the three bitmaps joined.

Toggle the guides off by choosing View | Guides | Show Guides. This will enable you to see the seams.

6 Select the Blur tool in the Tool panel. In the Properties Inspector, set its size to 20 and its intensity to 90. Blur the top and left edges of the original tile so that they blend well with the two duplicate tiles.

You might need to use the Brush tool to add more patches to help blend the edges. The idea is to adjust the original tile portion so that it will seamlessly blend into adjacent copies.

Toggle the guides back on by choosing View | Guides | Show Guides.

7 Select the Marquee tool and draw a selection about 30 pixels wide over the right edge of the original tile. Delete the selected area. Move the selection over to same relative spot on the left tile. Hold down the Option+Cmd (Mac) or Alt+Ctrl (PC) keys and drag a copy of the selected area back to the original tile.

8 Repeat this process to patch up the bottom edge. Draw a selection over the bottom portion of the original tile and delete. Move the selection up to the top tile and grab a copy of its bottom to move back down to the original tile.

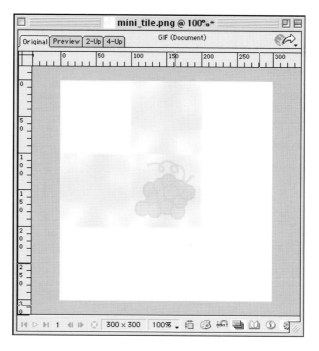

Create two copies of the parchment bitmap and place them at the top and left edges of the original.

Tip: Concentrate your touchup airbrushing and blending on the original tile portion—it is the only portion you will ultimately keep. If your touchups are too heavy on the two tile copies, your tile will not be seamless.

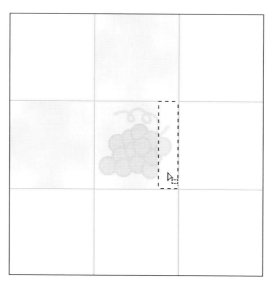

Select the right edge of the original tile and delete.

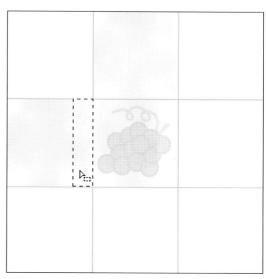

Move the selection to the left tile to grab its right edge for copying.

9 After you've patched up the original tile, draw a selection around it using the guides to help you. Choose Edit | Crop Document. Select the parchment graphic with the Pointer tool and, in the Layers panel (or in the Properties Inspector), adjust its opacity to 50%.

Your selection over the original tile should snap to the guides you set up earlier.

10 Choose File | Save As and save your tile as **mini_tile.png** to your desktop. To export it as a GIF ready for the web, in the Optimize panel, leave the Optimization settings at Gif WebSnap 128. Choose File | Export. In the Export window, choose Images Only from the Save As options. Save the file as **mini_tile.gif** to your desktop. Quit Fireworks.

Saving to the desktop will help you find the file again in later steps.

You should now have saved on your desktop a PNG version, which you'll use as a custom Fireworks pattern, and a GIF version that's ready for the web.

11 Locate the Configuration folder within the Fireworks folder on your computer. Place the PNG version of the tile inside the Patterns folder within the Configuration folder. Restart Fireworks.

Crop the tile down to its original shape and adjust its transparency in the Layers panel.

Tip: Instead of saving your pattern to the Configurations folder as you did in the previous section, you can simply save the file on your desktop or in a project folder and then point to it through the Pattern Options window. Select Other from the Pattern options pop-up instead of choosing one from the list and navigate to your file's location. By choosing Other and navigating to a file, the effect is the same. What you lose, however, is the convenience of having your custom tile as one of the pattern options in Fireworks the next time you work.

SIMULATING THE FINAL WEB PAGE LOOK

Now that you've exported your tile as a GIF ready for the web, the next step is to actually build your web page layout. In this section, you'll start a new document and fill the canvas with your new custom background tile pattern. This way, as you build your web page design, you'll be able to see how your designs will look when superimposed on the tiled pattern. After building a web page design, the background tile will help you select a matte color for your graphics so that, when you export design elements as transparent GIFs, they'll match the background tile.

1 In Fireworks, create a new document that is 800×600 pixels, 72dpi, with a transparent background. Use the Rectangle tool to draw a rectangle. With the Properties Inspector, size the rectangle to exactly 800×600 and position it at X = 0, Y = 0 so that it is the exact size as the canvas.

2 In the Properties Inspector, change the rectangle's fill from Solid to Pattern in the pop-up menu. Click the mini pattern swatch to open the Pattern Options window. From there, select your **mini_tile.png** file from the pop-up list of choices. Double-click the layer and name it **Tile**. Lock the **Tile** layer and create a new layer for your design elements.

The document now fills with your seamless tile pattern. The effect is the same as an HTML page that uses a background tile. You can now design your page in Fireworks, knowing what it will look like against an HTML background tile.

3 Choose File | Import and browse to locate the **art_wine_logo.png** file included in the **Project 4** folder on the accompanying CD-ROM. Click to place the logo in your design and position it in the upper-left corner of the document.

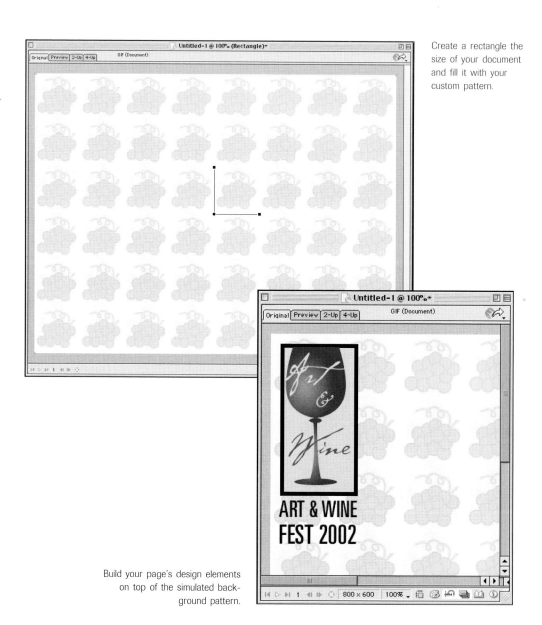

Create a rectangle the size of your document and fill it with your custom pattern.

Build your page's design elements on top of the simulated background pattern.

4 In the Optimize panel, select the GIF Adaptive setting with 128 Colors. Change the transparency to Alpha Transparency in the pop-up menu. For Matte, click the color swatch and then move the cursor over to your document. Sample a gray color (like #CCCCCC) from your background tile, such as the grayish color at the edge of one of the grapes.

> **Note:** Whenever you use background tiles, it's important to prepare your graphics as transparent GIFs with a matte color (edge color) that matches the median color value of your tile. Once loaded into a web browser, it's impossible to predict where the tiled pattern will fall relative to your images. Therefore, you cannot export your graphics presuperimposed onto the tile.

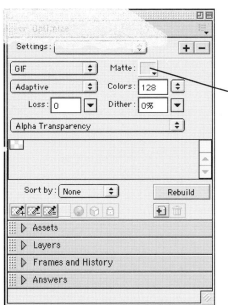

Select GIF Adaptive and 128 Colors, turn on Alpha Transparency, and set your Matte to a color from the background tile.

Select a Matte color

5 In the Layers panel, turn off the background tile's layer. Select the Export Area tool in the Tool panel. (It is grouped behind the Crop tool.) Draw a selection around the masthead design and press the Enter or Return key to export the region.

In the Export Preview window, all of your settings from the previous step should be reflected—just click Export. Save the file as **masthead.gif**. You now have both the background tile GIF and the masthead GIF that you need to start building this web page in an HTML editor like Dreamweaver.

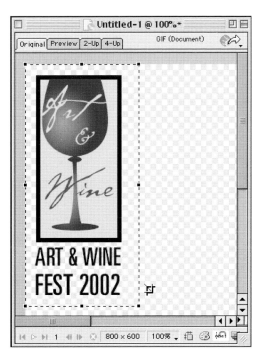

Turn off the layer with the tiled pattern and use the Export Area tool to export the logo.

OPTIMIZING AND EXPORTING AN OVERSIZED TILE

So far, this project has discussed building and using a small tile that repeats across the page, creating a seamless pattern. Web page background tiles, however, do not need to be a certain size. In fact, they could be just 2×1,500 pixels if you wanted users to see a horizontal pattern repeating down the page but not across it (unless they scrolled way off the page to see it, of course). In this final section, you'll create a single, large, 1,500×1,500-pixel tile that will add tremendous depth to your page without taking forever to download. The tile is large enough that users will not see it repeat unless they purposefully scroll to see it.

1 In Fireworks, create a new file that is 1,500×1,500 pixels, 72dpi, with a dark blue background (#000066).

2 With the Ellipse tool, draw an oval, fill it with white, use no stroke. With the Properties Inspector or Info panel, size it to be 1,904 pixels wide by 2,232 pixels high. Position it to X = 112, Y = −164.

> **Tip:** It helps to zoom out to 25% so you can see the entire design.

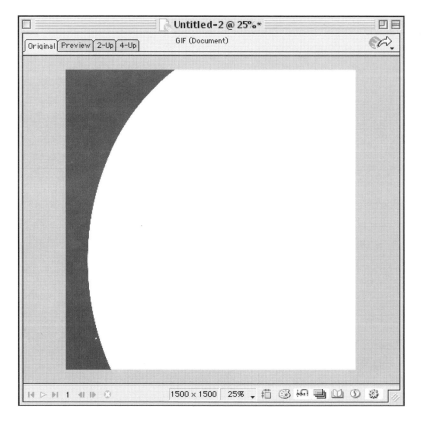

Create a large document and add an oval. This design will form the basis of your tile.

3 Choose File | Import and browse to the **compass.png** file included in the **Project 4** folder on the accompanying CD-ROM. Click once to place the image in your document. Use the Info panel to position it to X = 201, Y = –71.

4 Open the Optimize panel, select the GIF Adaptive palette, and enter **6** for the number of Colors. Set the transparency to No Transparency.

Click the Preview tab at the top of the document to preview the results. Though the image is 1,500×1,500 pixels, it is only 37KB because it uses so few colors. Click back to the Original tab.

> **Note:** Although 37KB might still be a fairly large image, if not many other graphics are added to the web page, you can still get good download performance. Always design pages that perform well for the connection speeds of the target audience.

5 Choose File | Export from the menu. In the Export window, choose Images Only from the Save As options. Name the file **big_tile.gif** and save it to your desktop (where it will be easy to find again).

6 To use either your large or small tile as the background for an HTML page, open Dreamweaver and start a new page. Choose Modify | Page Properties. Click the Browse button next to the Background Image field. Locate either one of your tiles and click OK.

The image will now serve as the background pattern for your web page. You can continue to add elements like text and tables to the page as usual.

> **Note:** To embed a tile in a web page, if you do not have Dreamweaver, you can open an HTML page in a text editor and add the background attribute to the body tag. For example, expand the <body> tag as follows: `<body background="tile.gif">`.

Import and place the **compass.png** file. This document is shown at 25%.

In Dreamweaver, you can specify the background tile of a page through the Page Properties window.

MODIFICATIONS

Instead of building background tiles—large or small—for the entire web page, you can build them for individual table cells. If you use a table structure as part of your web page layout, each cell within the table is capable of holding its own unique background tile. By using table cell tiles, you gain infinite control of your page's look and feel.

> **Note:** For this final section, you will need to use Dreamweaver. If you do not have Dreamweaver, you can add background tiles to your table cells by expanding the `<td>` tag as follows:
>
> `<td background="bgtile.gif">`

1 In Fireworks, open **tablecell_tile.png** from the **Project 4** folder on the accompanying CD-ROM. The file contains designs for a simple masthead and logo.

The text portion has already been exported for you and is located in the **Project 4** folder on the accompanying CD-ROM as **captain.gif**. In this section, you will export the horizontal stripes as a background tile that you can insert into a Dreamweaver table cell.

2 Select the top slice object covering the horizontal lines. Hold down the Control key (Mac) or right-click (PC) the slice and choose Export Selected Slice from the pop-up Context menu.

Note that the slice has already been optimized in the Optimize panel.

3 In the Export window, choose Images Only from the Save As options. Next to Slices, make sure the Selected Slice Only option is checked. Name the file **tablecell_tile.gif** and save it to your desktop (where you can find it again easily).

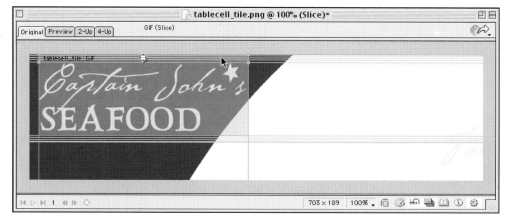

Build your web designs in a Fireworks layer on top of the background tile. Use slices to export your design elements like the horizontal lines.

> **Note:** If you click the slice object for the text portion and look in the Optimize panel, you'll notice that the slice is using Index Transparency and a dark blue matte that matches the underlying tile. Before exporting this slice, however, I had to turn off the underlying tile layer so that it wasn't included in the graphic. You'll prepare the horizontal line graphic in the same way.

4 Launch Dreamweaver and open the **captain.htm** file included in the **Project 4** folder on the accompanying CD-ROM.

5 Click inside the top cell above the text. In the Properties Inspector, click the folder icon to the right of the Bg text field. Locate your **tablecell_tile.gif** on the desktop and click OK.

Note: When using background tiles in table cells, always check your pages in multiple web browsers to make sure they are working correctly.

6 Cmd+click or right-click in the bottom cell of the table below the text. In the Properties Inspector, click the folder icon and browse to the **tablecell_tile.gif** file to make it the background pattern for the lower cell as well.

7 To preview your work, choose File | Preview in Browser (or press F12). Your page will open in a web browser.

Notice that if you resize your browser window, the horizontal lines always stretch completely across the page. Also, because the tile is a transparent GIF, it looks good on top of both the blue and white areas.

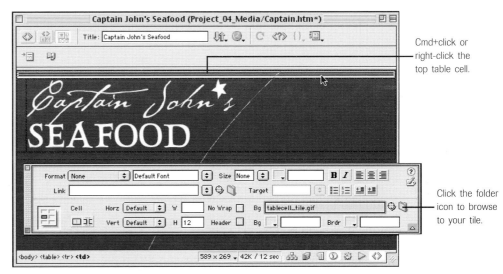

Cmd+click or right-click the top table cell.

Click the folder icon to browse to your tile.

Use the Properties Inspector to browse to a background file for the selected table cell.

This page uses one background tile for the whole page and a different tile to fill two table cells.

ANIMATED PRODUCT

SHOWCASE

"Luck is a matter of preparation

meeting opportunity."

—OPRAH WINFREY

BUILDING A DYNAMIC INTERFACE WITH ROLLOVER ANIMATIONS

I am continually amazed at how few web

design and production firms have discovered

the ease of use and magic of Fireworks for

building dynamic graphical interfaces. Without

writing a single line of code or having to

switch back and forth from one program to

another, you can build interactive rollover

buttons that trigger animations—all in a single

Fireworks document.

Animated Product Showcase

by Lisa Lopuck

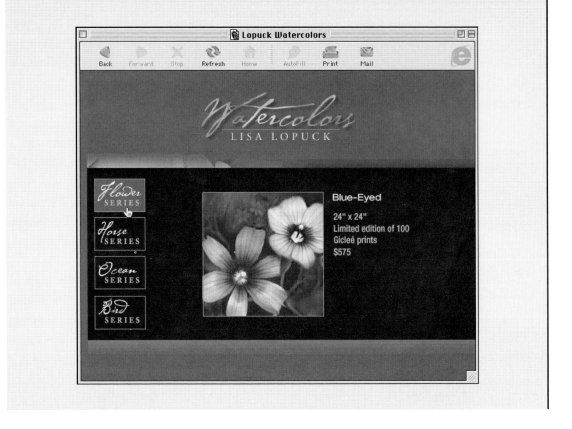

GETTING STARTED

Fireworks PNG documents are multidimensional. Like Photoshop, Fireworks enables you to build your graphics in a series of layers. Fireworks, however, goes one step further than Photoshop by offering a timeline in the form of frames. In the Frames panel, you build the different states of your rollover buttons and your animation steps. For example, the normal button state goes on Frame 1, and the rollover state goes on Frame 2. Animation steps can use any number of frames, and you don't necessarily have to start your animation on the first frame. In this project, you'll build a multistate, interactive button that triggers an animated product showcase.

BUILDING A BUTTON

To create an interactive button that can trigger an animation to appear, you begin by
building a few different button states in a series of frames. After building the buttons'
states, you then slice the region with the Slice tool, apply behaviors to it, and assign a
link. In this first section, you'll prepare the necessary frames for a two-state button—
a button that has a normal and a rollover state.

1 In Fireworks, open the **watercolors.png** file included
in the **Project 5** folder on the accompanying CD-
ROM. The left side of the page contains a vertical
row of buttons that you'll turn into rollover buttons.

2 In the Frames panel, hold down the Option or Alt
key and click Frame 1. This action creates a duplicate
of the first frame. Click Frame 2 to select it.

3 On Frame 2, Shift+select all four gray outlines
around the buttons. In the Properties Inspector,
change the fill color of the rectangles from None to
dark gray #333333 and the stroke color to white.

You've just made the rollover states for the four
buttons. Rollover states always go on Frame 2.

Select the four button
rectangles, set their stroke
to white, and fill them with
a dark gray color.

4 Select the Slice tool and draw slices over each of the four buttons. Make sure you draw your slice objects from the left edge of the document and draw your slices so that they all touch, leaving no gaps between them. Also make sure their right edges line up.

When you draw a slice, you are creating a table structure. If you leave gaps between your slices, Fireworks will create additional slices between them, creating a table that is more complex than necessary.

5 Shift+select all four slice objects. Open the Optimize panel and select the GIF format, Adaptive palette, and 16 Colors. Deselect the slice objects.

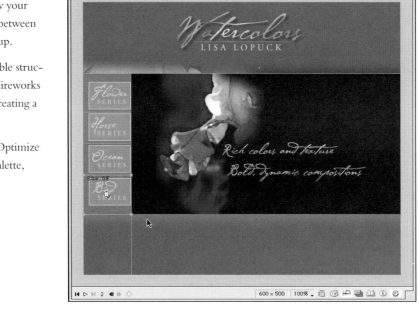

Draw four slices to cover each of the buttons. Make sure your slices line up to one another, edge to edge.

6 Select the top slice for the Flower Series button. In the Properties Inspector, enter the link **flower.htm** and press the Return or Enter key to make the link "stick." In the lower left of the Properties Inspector, rename the slice **Nav_1** and press the Return or Enter key. Repeat this step to add a link and name the remaining three buttons as follows:

Button 2: **horse.htm**, **Nav_2**

Button 3: **ocean.htm**, **Nav_3**

Button 4: **bird.htm**, **Nav_4**

7 Shift+select all four slice objects and open the Behavior panel. From the Plus (+) menu, select the Simple Rollover behavior.

This behavior will reveal the contents of Frame 2 when the user rolls over the buttons. Save your file as **watercolors_(yourname).png** to your desktop.

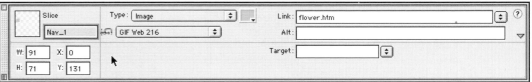

Select each slice and, in the Properties Inspector, name it and add a link.

ANIMATING OBJECTS

Fireworks is a full-featured animation program complete with tools to automatically generate animation frames and control looping and timing. In this section, you'll build and export a product animation that you can display when the user rolls over the top-left navigation button. Though this project walks you through the creation of just one button's rollover animation, you can use these same techniques to build a similar animation for each of the buttons—all in one Fireworks document.

1 In Fireworks, open the **watercolors2.png** file included in the **Project 5** folder on the accompanying CD-ROM or continue working with your project. Select Frame 2 in the Frames panel, click the flower image, and delete it.

2 Choose File | Import and locate the **painting1.png** file in the **Project 5** folder. Click once to place the **painting1.png** file in your document. While the painting is selected, choose Modify | Group. In the Properties Inspector, position the group to X = 200, Y = 170.

3 While the painting is selected, choose Modify | Animation | Animate Selection. In the Animation window, use the following settings and click OK:

Frames: **3**

Movement: **0**

Opacity: **20%** to **100%**

When you click OK, a dialog box asks if Fireworks can add more frames. Click OK.

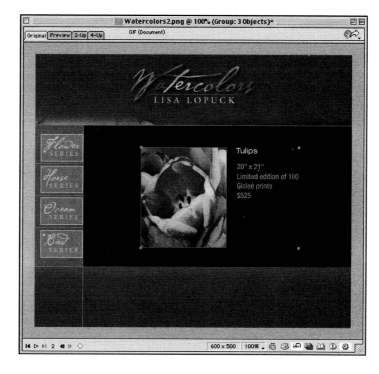

Import art onto Frame 2 of the **watercolors2.png** interface.

4 Click Frame 4 in the Frames panel to select it. To the right of the name "Frame 4," you'll see a number 7. This number determines the frame's delay in hundredths of a second. Double-click the number 7 and enter **300** in the pop-up text field. Press the Enter or Return key.

Entering 300 will make the frame delay three seconds.

5 While Frame 4 is selected, click the New/Duplicate Frame icon at the bottom of the Frames panel (to the left of the Trash icon). Click the new Frame 5 to select it. (You will have to double-click its frame delay to reset it back to 7.) Choose File | Import. Navigate to **painting2.png** and click once to place it in your document.

6 While the painting is selected, choose Modify | Group. Use the Properties Inspector to position it to X = 200, Y = 170. Choose Modify | Animation | Animate Selection. Use the same settings you used for the earlier painting and click OK. Fireworks will ask you if it's okay to add more frames; click OK. Double-click the frame delay number on Frame 7 and change it to **300**.

Note: Fireworks behaves better if you use the sliders to adjust the Movement to **0** in the Animate Selection window. If you type a value in, sometimes Fireworks ignores it.

---

7 Click the New/Duplicate Frame icon to add a new frame (reset the frame delay back to 7). Repeat steps 3 through 6 to import and animate **painting3.png** and **painting4.png**.

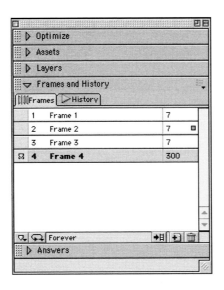

Double-click the number next to the frame's name to set its delay.

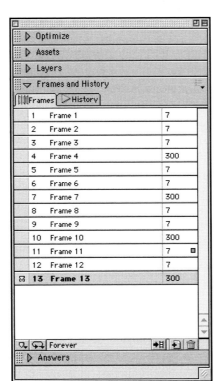

After importing and animating all four paintings, your Frames panel should look like this.

EXPORTING GIF ANIMATIONS

As you saw in the preceding section, Fireworks enables you to control the interframe delay of your animation. Fireworks also enables you to control which frames you want to include in an animation and whether the frames loop endlessly or play through one or more times before stopping. In this section, you'll adjust the Frames panel to export an animated GIF of selected frames.

1 Continue working with your file or open **watercolors3.png**. Select Frame 1. Frame 1 shows the widest possible area that all the art will occupy. Draw a slice over the image. Click Frames 4, 7, 10, and 13 to make sure your slice does not accidentally exclude any of the painting art.

2 While the slice is selected, open the Optimize panel and choose the Animated GIF format, Adaptive palette, and 256 Colors.

3 In the Frames panel, double-click Frame 1's delay (the number 7). In the pop-up window, uncheck the Include When Exporting option. A red X will appear where the number 7 was, indicating that Frame 1 will not be included in the animation when you export.

Excluding frames is your way of building multiple animations in one Fireworks document and then exporting just one animation at a time. You can specify which frames to exclude for each individually selected slice object.

4 As of now, the animation will loop (replay) continuously. To change this so that the animation plays through only once, click and hold down the looping icon (the second icon from the lower left). Select 1 from the pop-up list.

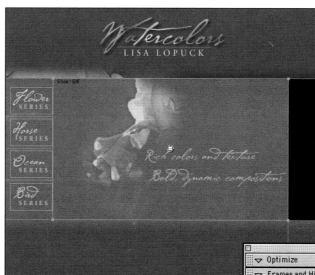

Draw a slice to cover the image. Make sure your slice does not clip the paintings on Frames 4, 7, 10, and 13.

Double-click a frame to access controls that enable you to exclude it from the animation.

5 Make sure the central slice over the animation is selected and choose File | Export. In the Export window, choose Images Only from the Save As options. For Slices, choose the Export Slices option. Most importantly, check the Selected Slices Only option. Name the file **flowers.gif**, navigate to a folder where you'll find it once you save it, and click Save.

6 Now that you've exported the animation, you can add a Swap Image behavior to the topmost Flowers Series button. Select the top Flowers Series button. Click the slice's central target icon and drag it over to the large painting slice. Let go when you see a thin blue line connecting the two slices. After you let go, a pop-up window will appear asking what image to use in the swap.

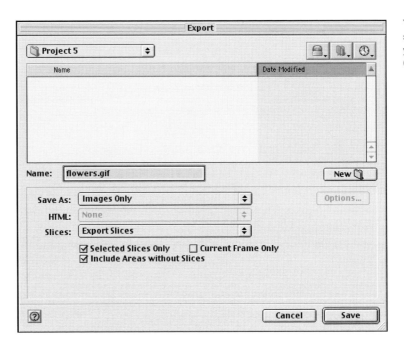

You can export a selected slice within your document if you check the Selected Slices Only option.

7 Click the More Options button on the Swap Image window. In the window that appears, select the Image File option and then click the Folder icon to navigate to your saved **flowers.gif** animation. Click OK.

Now, when the user rolls over the Flowers Series button, the animation you just exported will appear in the central sliced area.

8 Now that you've exported the center slice as an animation, you must exclude the animation frames before exporting the page. The easiest way to do this is to select the central slice and, in the Optimize panel, change the setting from Animated GIF to plain old GIF format. Also, double-click Frame 1 and check the Include When Exporting box.

When you set up a Swap Image behavior, you can decide to swap in either a static image or an animated GIF file.

9 Choose File | Export from the menu and, in the Export window, choose HTML and Images from the Save As options. Make sure Export Slices is selected from the Slices options and check the Put Images in Subfolder option. This option neatly places all the sliced graphics into a folder. Name the file **index.html** and click Save.

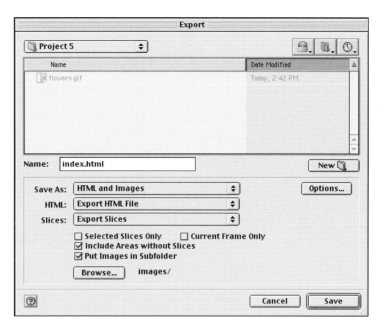

Export the entire page as HTML and Images with Export Slices turned on.

10 Locate your exported **index.html** file and open it in a browser to preview. Note that you can also preview your work in a browser right from Fireworks before you export. To do so, choose File | Preview in Browser and select your browser of choice.

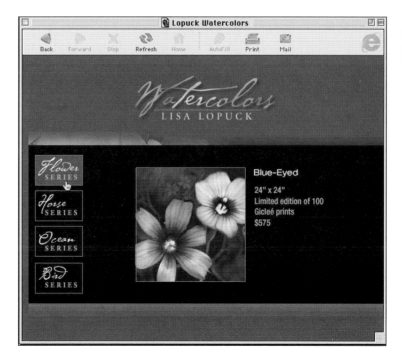

Upon rolling over the top Flower Series button, you'll see your animation appear in the center.

MODIFICATIONS

In this project, you explored Fireworks's live animation effects, whereby you can select any object—bitmap or vector—and choose Modify | Animation | Animate Selection. This technique is a way to create an instant animation that you can change quickly by adjusting its parameters in the Properties Inspector. Another way to animate objects in Fireworks, however, is to use the Tween feature. The Tween feature essentially takes a beginning state and an ending state and figures out a number of steps in between. In this last section, you'll use Fireworks's Tween feature to animate a drop shadow effect moving from one side to the other side of an object.

1 In Fireworks, start a new document that is 400×400 pixels and has a white background.

2 Choose File | Import and locate **painting1.png** in the **Project 5** folder on the accompanying CD-ROM. Click once to place the painting in the document.

Place the **painting1.png** file into a new document with a white background.

3 Select the painting and its outline and choose Modify | Symbol | Convert to Symbol. In the dialog box, name the symbol **painting** and select the Graphic option. Click OK.

The painting is technically now an "instance" of the symbol.

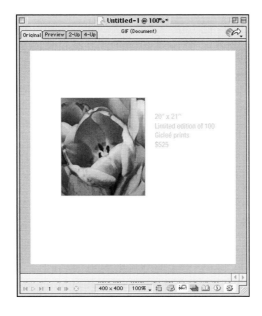

4 In the Properties Inspector, click the Plus (+) sign icon and select the Shadow and Glow | Drop Shadow option. Use the following settings:

Distance: **22**

Angle: **320°**

Leave all other settings at their defaults and then click outside the small window to close it.

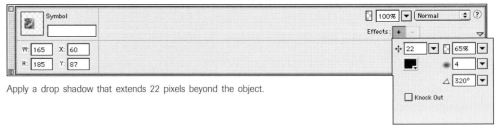

Apply a drop shadow that extends 22 pixels beyond the object.

5 Copy the painting instance and paste. It will paste in place. While the copy is selected, choose Drop Shadow Effect again from the Properties Inspector to make some adjustments. Make the distance **22** pixels and set the angle to **225°**. Click outside the small window to close it.

6 Select both instances. (You can do this by dragging your cursor over the painting or by Shift+selecting both instances in the Layers panel.) Choose Modify | Symbol | Tween Instances. In the dialog box, enter **10** frames and check the Distribute to Frames option. Click OK.

You've just created a Tweened animation. The first symbol instance becomes Frame 1, and the copied instance becomes the last frame. Fireworks added 8 frames in between the starting and ending point for a total of 10 frames.

7 To preview your animation, click the Play button at the bottom left of the document window.

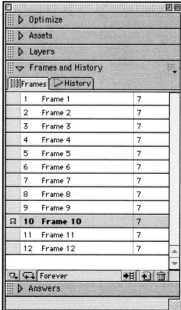

After building an animation, you can preview it in the document by clicking the Play button.

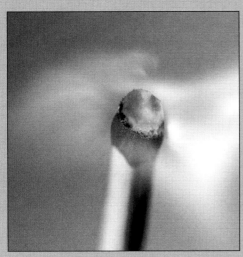

DYNAMIC INTERFACE

DESIGN

"There is no excellent beauty that hath not

some strangeness in the proportion."

—FRANCIS BACON

USING ROLLOVERS TO MAGICALLY EXPAND YOUR PAGE'S INTERFACE

An interactive site will keep your viewers

entertained and can provide clarity and

incentive to navigational choices. In web pages,

where space is always an issue, remote

rollovers (often called disjoint or swap rollovers)

can be used to trigger new content in a

reusable location. When that content is

animated, your site can really deliver!

Project 6

Dynamic Interface Design

by Donna Casey

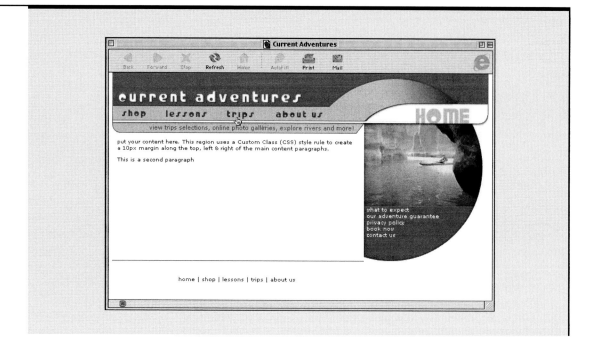

GETTING STARTED

Through the use of simple animation symbols and masked photos, you'll create a navigation system that uses hotspots to trigger remote rollovers in two different areas of the page layout. To help you focus on the interactive elements, the page layout has been set up and preorganized.

You will be working with the file **ca_start.png** in the **Project 6** folder on the accompanying CD-ROM. Before you begin, install the fonts (Crystal Radio Kit) found in the **Fonts** folder. These are just some of the many free fonts found at **www.larabiefonts.com**.

BUILDING THE TAB GRAPHIC SYMBOL

Before you begin this project, take a look at the finished file (**ca_final.png**) on the accompanying CD-ROM to get an idea of what you will build. Use a browser to open **site_final.htm** from the **Finished_site** folder inside the **Project 6** folder. Move your mouse over the four section choices to see the remote rollover effects.

Each hotspot triggers an animated tab element that provides additional information about each section of the site. In this part of the project, you'll build the tab shape in the page layout and convert it to a graphic symbol. The Library panel of **ca_start.png** contains a sample tab element (**submenu_sample**) that can be used if you want to skip building the tab shape.

1 Open **ca_start.png** from the **Project 6** folder. In the Layers panel, select the **menu animations** layer to make it active. You can lock and hide all the layers to give you enough room to work.

Using layers to organize your elements and control their positioning can be critical to the success of your layout. In this case, all the animated tab elements will be placed on the **menu animations** layer. The elements in the layers above lay on top of the tab animations to provide depth to the design.

2 Use the Rounded Rectangle tool (click and hold on the Rectangle tool to reveal the Rounded Rectangle tool) to draw a box that is 490×40. Use the Properties Inspector to position the element at exactly 0,73. Press Enter to snap the rectangle to the location coordinates. This rectangle will ultimately become one of your tabbed buttons after you make modifications to it.

Note: Fireworks now uses the Properties Inspector to provide the settings formerly found only in the Info panel. These settings, however, can also be found in the Info panel in the Window menu.

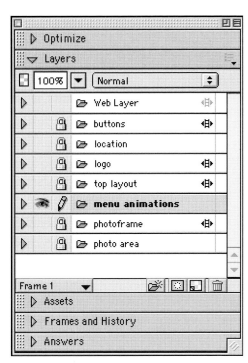

Layers help you control which elements will overlap others in your rollover animations.

3 In the Properties Inspector, give the rectangle a single-pixel blue (#003366) stroke along its edge. Set the Fill to green (#99FF66).

4 With the Rectangle selected, use the Properties Inspector to set the Rectangle Roundness property to 80%. Choose Modify | Ungroup.

Rectangles are grouped by default to make the corners editable. If you ungroup, you no longer can adjust the corner radius. Ungrouping, however, enables you to edit the rectangle's anchor points.

Note: Using the Scale tool to change the width or height of your rectangle can adversely affect the corner radius. Also your rectangle is twice the height needed because you will cut it and use only the bottom half.

5 Unlock and turn on the visibility of the **photo area** layer if you've turned it off. Switch to the Knife tool. See the anchor points for the rectangle's path? With the Shift key pressed to constrain your cut, horizontally drag the Knife tool completely across the rounded rectangle right at the top level of the photograph.

6 Switch to the Subselection tool and Shift+click the bottom half of the rectangle to deselect it. Use the Delete key to get rid of the top half that is still selected.

7 To make the remaining half into a completed path, select the Pen tool and click once on the upper-left point. Then click the upper-right path.

When you deleted the top portion, you left an open path of the half rectangle. The stroke, therefore, did not continue along the top line.

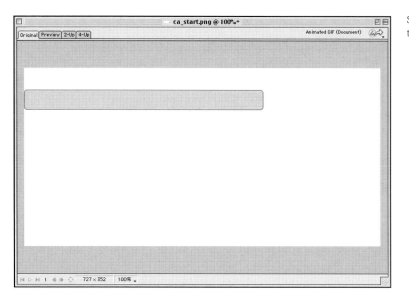

Start with a regular rectangle to build a tab shape.

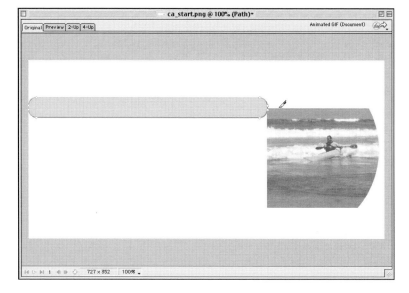

Hold down the Shift key to create a perfect horizontal cut.

Note: You can use the Command (Mac) or Control (PC) key to temporarily switch from your current tool to a selection tool. Depending on your active tool, this will switch you to either the Selection or Subselection tool.

8 With the Subselection tool, alter the right corner to be straight instead of curved. Click the lower-right point to reveal its Beziér handles. Click the handle and drag it back to the point.

9 When finished, select the tab element and choose Modify | Symbol | Convert to Symbol. Select Graphic Symbol and name it **tab_default**.

In the Layers panel, name the instance of your new symbol after its x,y coordinates 0,73. After you create a symbol, the symbol itself lives in the Library panel. What you see in your document is an *instance*, or copy, of the symbol.

10 Choose File | Save As and save the file as **myca.png**.

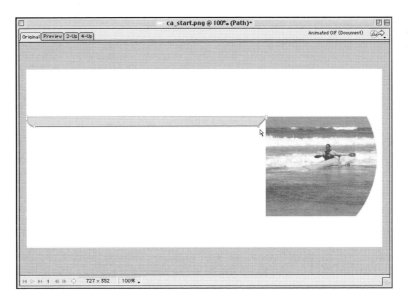

Use the Subselection tool to straighten the curved path.

CREATING THE MOUSEOUT ANIMATIONS

Now that you've built the basic tab shape, the next step is to animate it using Fireworks's Tween feature. *Tweening* is the process of automatically building an animation based on a starting point and an ending point that you define. With tweening, you'll create the MouseOut stage of your animated rollovers (what the tab does when the user rolls off of it). In the MouseOut stage, the tab will animate upward so that it is hidden under the main navigation bar.

1 Continue working with your saved file or open **ca_1.png** from the **Project 6** folder. Open the Library panel and select the tab_default graphic. From the Library panel's options, choose Duplicate and then double-click the new symbol to open the Symbol Properties window. Change its type to Animation Symbol. Change its name to **shoptab_up**.

2 While still in the Symbol Properties window, click the Edit button to open the Symbol Editor window. Select the Text tool. Before you begin typing, adjust your settings in the Properties Inspector to the following: right-aligned, 12 point, dark blue (#003366) text. Click on the middle right area of the tab to begin typing.

3 Type **Shop for gear, from rafts and kayaks to the very latest in accessories!** and make sure to position the text just above the bottom-right anchor point of the tab.

Note: Symbols have their own unique set of layers and frames apart from the main document.

4 Select the new text and the tab element, choose Modify | Group, and then choose Modify | Symbol | Convert to Symbol. Accept the default settings and name the Graphic Symbol **shoptab**.

The symbol is now created in the Library. Any occurrence of a symbol within another symbol (as is the case here) or on the canvas is called an instance.

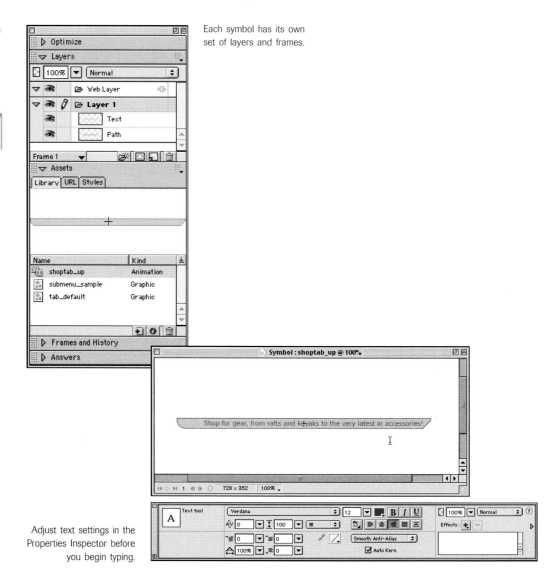

Each symbol has its own set of layers and frames.

Adjust text settings in the Properties Inspector before you begin typing.

5 In the Symbol Editor window, create a duplicate of the shoptab instance by choosing Edit | Copy | Paste. Position the duplicate exactly 20 pixels above the original by holding down the Shift key and pressing the up arrow on your keyboard twice.

With two copies, or instances, of a symbol, you can ask Fireworks to create an instant animation by adding a number of steps in between the two. The first instance establishes the starting point, and the second one marks the ending point. "Tweening" is the process of figuring out the steps between the starting and ending points.

Tip: You can use the Shift key with the Page Up Arrow to move an element 10 pixels at a time.

6 Shift+select both instances of the shoptab symbol and choose Modify | Symbol | Tween Instances. Enter **2** steps and check the Distribute to Frames option. Click OK.

The number of steps you choose equals the number of steps that will be added *between* the starting and ending instances. The Distribute to Frames option will add enough frames to your file to place each instance on a separate frame. The original instance will exist on the first frame. The copied instance will be placed on the last frame. The stepped instances will be added to the frames in between.

7 Close the Symbol Editor window to return to your document. From the Library panel, drag an instance of the shoptab_up animation to the canvas. Place it on the **menu animations** layer. Click OK to add the frames needed for the animation when the dialog box appears.

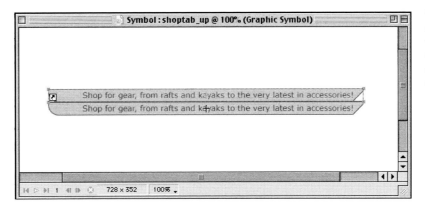

To create a tweened animation, you need two copies of a symbol instance—a starting position and an ending position.

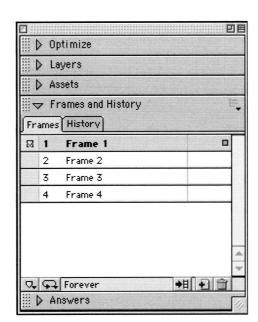

The Tween function adds animation steps between a starting and an ending symbol instance.

8 While in Frame 1, use the Properties Inspector to position the animation at 0,73. Save your file.

You can move the animation from any frame in your document, and all frames will be repositioned properly. Step through the animation using the controls along the bottom of the document window to see the tab slide up under the site's framework. This animation will be the MouseOut action when the user rolls off one of the navigation buttons.

9 To create the remaining animations for the Lessons, Trips, and About Us buttons, select the original shoptab_up symbol in the Library panel and choose Duplicate from the Options pull-down menu. Name the duplicate **lessonstab_up**.

10 Double-click the lessonstab_up symbol to edit it. In the Frames panel, turn on Onion Skinning from the lower-left pull-down menu. Choose Select | Select All to select all of the frames and then choose Modify | Symbol | Break Apart. The Break Apart command enables you to edit the text of the symbol. Turn off Onion Skinning in the Frames panel.

11 Choose Edit | Find and Replace. Select the Search Document and Find Text settings. In the Find field, enter the text from the shoptab_up symbol. In the Change To field, enter **Learn to paddle! We offer whitewater, sea & surf kayaking, and guide school.** Press the Replace All button. Close the Symbol Editor window

In the Library panel, create another duplicate of the shoptab_up symbol. Rename it **tripstab_up** and double-click it to edit it. Repeat steps 10 and 11 to turn it into the Trips tab. Repeat these steps again to build the About Us tab. When finished, save your file.

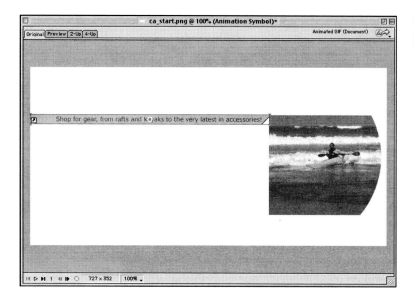

Position the animated symbol in your document on the **menu animations** layer.

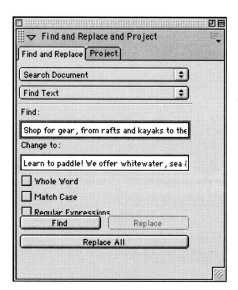

Use the Find and Replace window to update all frames of the animation symbol with new text.

BUILDING THE MOUSEOVER STATES

In this section, you'll build the MouseOver states (what the tabs look like when the user rolls over them). Using a duplicate of each tab animation you've already created, you will use a very cool built-in Fireworks command that reverses the upward motion of the animation.

1 Continue working with your saved file or open **ca_2.png** from the **Project 6** folder. Highlight the shoptab_up animation in the Library panel. From the panel options, choose Duplicate and double-click the new symbol to open its Properties and name it **shoptab_down**.

2 Click the Edit button to open the Symbol Editor window. Choose Commands | Document | Reverse Frames. In the Reverse Frames window, choose the All Frames options and click OK. Close the Symbol Editor window.

3 Repeat steps 1 and 2 to complete the three remaining MouseOver tab animations.

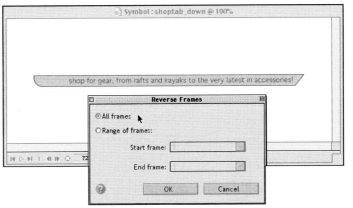

Select All Frames in the Reverse Frames dialog box.

4 Drag a copy of each MouseOver animation onto the workspace to Frame 1 of the **menu_animations** layer. Position each of the new MouseOver tab animations at 0,73 using the coordinate fields in the Properties Inspector. Save your file.

Drag each of the MouseOver animation symbols to the main document.

EXPORTING THE ANIMATIONS TO CREATE EXTERNAL FILES

When you create remote rollovers in Fireworks, a static image typically appears somewhere on the page when the user rolls over a button. Instead of displaying a static image, however, you can show an animation. To use the animations you've built so far in this project as swap rollovers, you must first export them as animated GIFs.

1 Continue with your saved file or open **ca_3.png** from the **Project 6** folder. Turn on the **Web** layer's visibility. Select the slice labeled tab_default (covering the tab animation area). The slice is optimized as an Animated GIF, using 16 colors with no dither.

2 In the Layers panel, turn off the Eye icon of the default tab graphic to hide it and make only one of the tab animations visible. Ctrl+click (Mac) or right-click (PC) on the tab_default slice to open a contextual menu. Choose Export Selected Slice from the menu.

3 In the Export dialog box, navigate to your desktop and create a new folder to contain the page. Name the folder **Site**. Inside the new **Site** folder, create another folder and name it **animations**.

The Export Settings should be Images Only, Selected Slices Only. Because you want to export all frames of your animation, uncheck the Current Frame Only option. Name the file according to the animation.

4 In the Layers panel, turn off the current animation and turn on a different one. Again, on the selected slice, right-click or ctrl+click and select Export Selected Slice from the context menu. In the Export Settings window, choose Images Only, Selected Slices Only, and disable the Current Frame Only option. Name and save the file.

5 Repeat this operation for the remaining animations. You should end up with four down animations and four up animations.

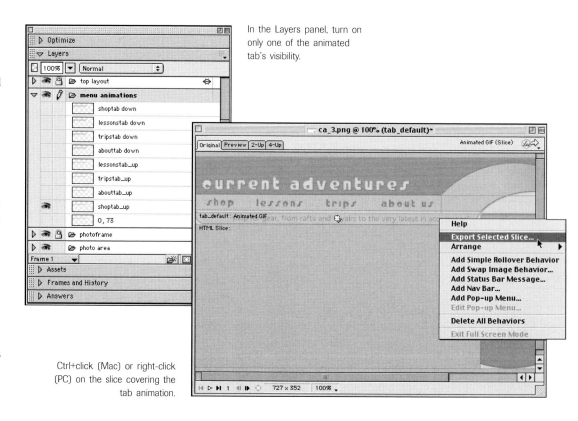

In the Layers panel, turn on only one of the animated tab's visibility.

Ctrl+click (Mac) or right-click (PC) on the slice covering the tab animation.

ADDING THE SWAP IMAGE BEHAVIORS

To build a working remote rollover in Fireworks, you must attach the Swap Image behavior to either a hotspot or a slice object. In this section, you will attach Swap Image behaviors to hotspots that not only will trigger the tab animation but also will switch out the photograph in the circle area.

1 Open **ca_4.png** in the **Project 6** folder. Ensure that the **Web** layer's visibility is turned on. Select the first hotspot over the Shop button. Click and drag the target-shaped icon on the hotspot over to the tab_default slice.

2 When the Swap Image dialog box appears, click the More Options button and then click the Folder icon to browse to an external file. Navigate to your **Site/ Animations** folder and select the **shoptab_down.gif** animation. Disable the Preload Images and Restore Image onMouseOut options.

3 Click and drag the central Target icon from the same hotspot, but this time drag to the photo slice.

4 In the Swap Image dialog box, again disable the Preload and Restore functions and then select the frame with the correct photo. In this case, the photo you want is on Frame 2.

Repeat these steps to set up remote rollover behaviors for the remaining buttons. They are completed for you in the **ca_5.png** file, although you might need to update the paths to the animated GIF files in each of the swap behaviors (depending on where you placed your animation folder).

5 Open **ca_5.png**. This file already has been prepared for export. Choose File | Export. In the Export window, name the file **interface.htm**, choose the HTML and Images option, and make sure Export Slices is selected from the pull-down menu. Check the Put Images in Subfolder option.

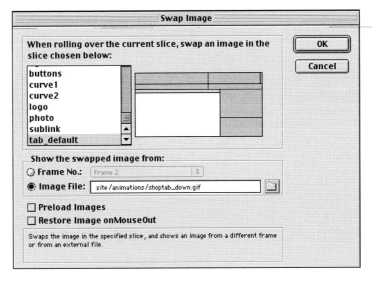

Choose a saved animated GIF file as the Swap Image source.

Note: When you use animation for a rollover, you should always disable the Preload Images option. Preloading caches the image before the page is presented to the user for viewing, resulting in an unpredictable starting frame. If you use preloading, you should try to keep your rollover files as small as possible so that they don't take forever to appear when the user mouses over interactive elements.

Using any instance of the Restore Image onMouseOut function would mean that all of the rollover effects would return to their original image onMouseOut. This would be okay for the photo, but it is not the plan for the tab element. Instead, you want to trigger the tab_up state onMouseOut. Unfortunately, Fireworks will not let you set separate behaviors for MouseOver and MouseOut. It assumes that only one Swap Image behavior is applied per targeted slice. This is a minor drawback that means you will have to complete your page in Dreamweaver, but don't worry—it's really easy!

6 Open the resulting file in a browser to preview your work. Most of the remote rollover functionality is there, but you'll need to go into Dreamweaver for final refinements. Remember that if your rollovers don't work, it's because the paths to the animated GIF files used in **ca_5.png** might be different than the path structure you have set up on your computer.

MODIFICATIONS

To finish your design, it's necessary to move to Dreamweaver. For example, the tabs currently animate out on MouseOver, but they do not animate back on MouseOut. This behavior is easily corrected in Dreamweaver.

1 Open the **interface.htm** file provided in the **Project 6** folder. This file is just like the one you exported, but it is updated with a background tile and a page title.

2 Select the hotspot over the shop portion of the button's image. Open the Behaviors panel and be sure that Show Events is set to 4.0 and Later Browsers. (You do this by clicking on the Plus (+) sign icon and selecting Show Events for | 4.0 and Later Browsers.)

3 Choose the Swap Image behavior from the Plus (+) sign icon Events drop-down list. When the dialog box appears, select tab_default from the list of Images and then click the Browse button to locate the **shoptab_up.gif** animation in the **Animations** folder. Uncheck the Preload and Restore options and click OK to keep your settings.

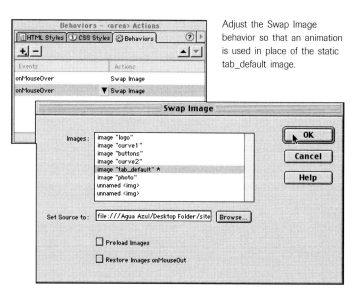

Adjust the Swap Image behavior so that an animation is used in place of the static tab_default image.

4 Change the second onMouseOver Event to onMouseOut in the Behaviors panel. (You do this by clicking on the down arrow to the left of the Swap Image text and selecting onMouseOut from the drop-down list.)

5 Repeat this process for each of the remaining hotspots. Each time, you will select the tab_default image but choose the correct animation for the hotspot selected. You will be using only the up versions of the animations. Remember to uncheck the Preload and Restore options each time.

6 Select the shop hotspot. In the Behaviors panel, double-click the onMouseOut Swap Image listing. Adjust the onMouseOut behavior to reset the central photo back to the original **photo.jpg** image when the mouse rolls off.

Highlight the photo image in the list and click the Browse button. Locate the **photo.jpg** image in the Images directory and click OK. Repeat these steps for the remaining hotspots.

7 Save your file and preview it in your browser.

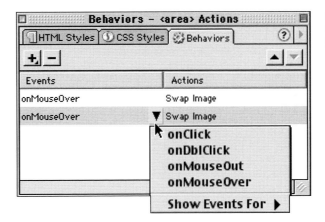

Change the mouse event from onMouseOver to onMouseOut in the Behaviors panel.

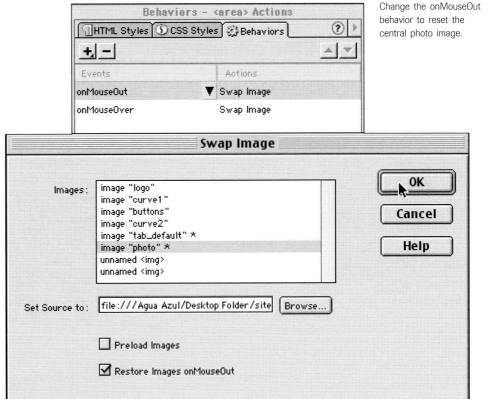

Change the onMouseOut behavior to reset the central photo image.

FLASHY BUTTONS

"To love what you do and feel that it matters—

how could anything be more fun?"

—KATHARINE GRAHAM
(FORMER PUBLISHER OF THE WASHINGTON POST)

BUILDING GREAT-LOOKING BUTTONS AND ART FOR FLASH MOVIES

Do you prefer drawing in Fireworks but want

to create custom buttons and animations in

Flash? Do you want to save time, minimize

frustration, and increase creativity? Then take

advantage of the ease of creating vector

artwork in Fireworks and combine it with the

superior vector animation capability of Flash

through the creation of an interactive animated

logo button.

Project 7

Flashy Buttons

by Abigail Rudner

GETTING STARTED

Realizing the power you possess when creating art with Fireworks, it is time to turn up the heat a bit and get things moving. In this project, you will explore the intricacies of Fireworks and Flash integration techniques. I will guide you through the creation of an interactive animated logo button and will touch on some powerful and effective methods for creating art and symbols and for exporting, importing, and modifying buttons and animation between Fireworks and Flash.

You will need Flash for this tutorial. You can download a 30-day trial of Flash from the Macromedia web site at **www.macromedia.com/software/flash**.

This tutorial assumes basic knowledge of Flash, including an understanding of the basic controls and how to work with frames, layers, and symbols. You also should understand how to save files and should know the difference between the FLA and SWF file formats.

DRAWING BUTTON AND MOVIE FRAME ARTWORK IN FIREWORKS

In this project, you'll learn how to create button art with vector illustration tools and how to customize the art with the Effects options in the Properties Inspector.

1   Start by creating a new file that's 70×70 pixels.
    Because you will be drawing a complex shape behind, which you might want the background to show, set your canvas color to transparent.

2 Select Frame 1 and draw a 24×24-pixel red circle with no stroke using the Circle tool from the Vector Shape tools. You can use the Info panel while you draw to measure as you drag. Place your circle in the middle of the canvas and fill it with red #FF0000 with no stroke.

This circle will become a button in Flash.

3 In the Properties Inspector, click the Effects | Bevel and Emboss | Inner Bevel button and apply the Inner Bevel effect with the following settings:

Edge type: Smooth
Width: 19
Contrast: 75
Angle: 135
Button Preset: Raised

Because the circle will become a button, the Inner Bevel effect gives it dimension to help make it look clickable.

4 Duplicate the frame two times by choosing Duplicate from the Frames panel Options menu.

It doesn't matter where in the stack you place the frames because they are all identical initially. You will now have three total frames, each with the circle button on it.

5 Name each of your frames as follows: Frame 1 = **Up**, Frame 2 = **Over**, Frame 3 = **Down**.

With the art on Frame 1 completed, you can now create the Star Blob on Frame 2. The Star Blob will be the rollover effect for your button.

Draw a red circle in the center of the canvas.

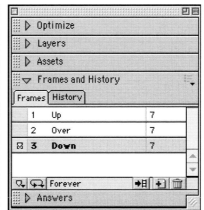

Three identical frames named Up, Over, and Down.

6 Select Frame 2 (the Over frame) and draw a small circle measuring approximately 8×8 pixels directly above the center circle.

7 Choose Clone from the Window menu to instantly copy and paste a duplicate of the new circle exactly on top of the first circle.

8 Select the Scale tool. Notice the black dot at the center of the selection. Click and drag to reposition it to the center point of the original circle. Now you can rotate it from this new center origin. Click and drag one of the corners to rotate the shape 72 degrees. You can open the Info panel from the Window menu to watch for feedback on the rotation degree as you drag.

9 Continue to clone and rotate the little circles by 72 degrees each until you have a total of five points.

Note: The Star Blob shape has five spokes that are rotated around the center circle. Because 360 divided by 5 equals 72, you will rotate each new circle around the center point 72 degrees.

10 Select all six circles that make up the Star Blob shape. Choose Modify | Combine Paths | Union.

You now have one shape instead of six, and the object inherits the effects from the original center circle. Frame 2 is now complete.

A small circle of approximately 8×8 pixels drawn directly above the center circle.

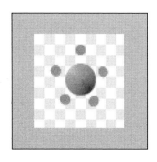

Clone and rotate the small circle five times.

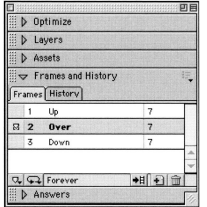

The finished Star Blob on Frame 2 with inherited effects.

MAKING THE "JUMPIN JACK"

In the next series of steps, you will create the jack shape for Frame 3.

1 Select Frame 3. Draw a small circle of approximately 12×12 pixels and a small vertical rectangle of approximately 5 pixels wide by 20 pixels high. Place both objects directly above the center circle in an arm-like configuration.

2 Make sure both parts of the arm are selected (but not the center circle). Choose Modify | Combine Paths | Union.

You now have one arm shape instead of two arm pieces.

3 Select Clone from the Modify menu to instantly copy and paste the shape in place on Frame 3.

4 Select the Scale tool. Reposition it to the center point of first circle and rotate it about 72 degrees. Continue this until you have created all five spokes of the jack.

5 Zoom in on the tips of the arm spokes and use the Subselection tool to select the tip points. Try tweaking and moving them manually or use the arrow keys on your keyboard so that some of the tip circles are larger than others.

Altering the circles by making some arms appear shorter and others longer will give the jack a little more personality. It is a little bit subtle but in the end will make a big difference.

The circle and rectangle placed directly above the center.

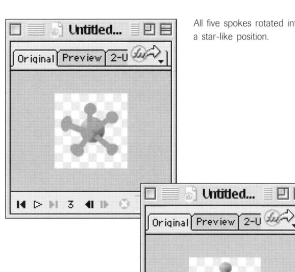

All five spokes rotated into a star-like position.

Unaltered spokes on the left compared to altered spokes with more personality on the right.

95

6 Select all the arms and the center circle and choose Modify | Combine Paths | Union to merge the parts. The object inherits the effects from the original center circle, and the jack shape and button frames are complete. Save your file as **jackbutton_fr03.png**.

Note: As an alternate to the artwork production method described so far, you can create a new button symbol in Fireworks and build the states of your button with the drawing tools directly inside the Fireworks Symbol Editor window. When your graphics are complete, keep the Symbol editor open and export it as a SWF file using the same steps.

EXPORTING THE BUTTON FRAMES FROM FIREWORKS

Now that the artwork for the three button states is complete, you are now entering what I call the "integrating zone." In this section, you will export the button frames that you created in Fireworks as a Flash SWF file. Once imported into Flash, you can make any further refinements you want to this art. This is the really cool stuff in Fireworks. Using Fireworks to create graphics and Flash to create interactivity enables you to optimize specific tasks in the application that suits each task best.

1 Choose File | Export Preview. In the window that appears, choose PNG 32 from the Format options.

Note: This setting is very important because it will ensure that your output will contain transparency and maintain its beveled appearance!

2 While in the Export Preview window, click the Export button. The Export dialog box displays. Choose Macromedia Flash SWF from the Save As options.

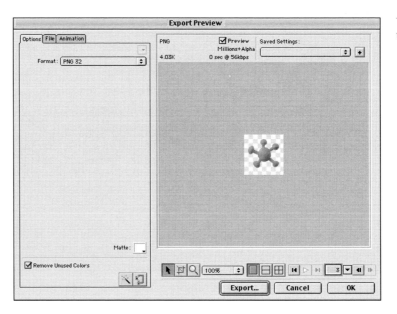

The Export Preview window with the PNG 32 Format selected.

3 Click the Options button and make sure the Maintain Appearance radio button is selected. Set JPEG Quality to 100, Frames to All, and Frame Rate to **20**. Click OK.

Save your file as **button_frames.swf**. To check your work, you also can view the **button_frames.swf** file in the **Project 7** folder on the accompanying CD-ROM.

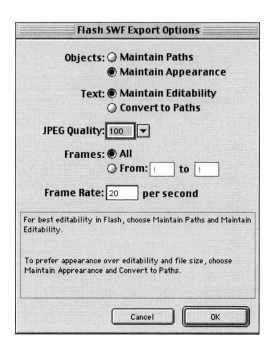

From the Export window, click the Options button to access this settings window for your SWF movie.

IMPORTING THE FIREWORKS BUTTON FRAMES INTO FLASH

In this section of the project, you'll import the Fireworks SWF button into Flash and turn it into a Flash button symbol. This symbol will then be incorporated into a Flash movie.

1 Launch Flash MX if it is not already open. Choose Modify | Movie and assign a Frame Rate of **20** fps, a Width of **300** pixels, and a Height of **200** pixels.

For this exercise, I kept Background Color set to white and Ruler Units set to Pixels.

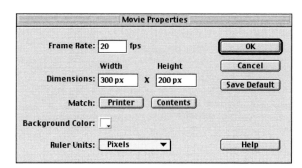

In the Movie Properties window, assign a Frame Rate of **20** fps, a Width of **300** pixels, and a Height of **200** pixels.

2 Choose Insert | New Symbol. Name your symbol **Jack Button** and click to select the Button Behavior option. Click OK.

The Button Symbol Editor window opens automatically.

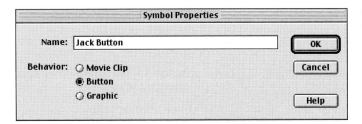

Create a new button symbol called **Jack Button**.

3 While in the Button Editor window, choose File | Import.

On the Macintosh, navigate to your **button_frames.swf** file in the **SWFs** folder, select it in the left pane, and click the Add button to move it to the right pane. Click the Import button.

In Windows, choose File | Import, browse into the **SWFs** folder, and select **button_frames.swf**.

Flash imports your Fireworks button and places each frame (or button state) on the appropriate Up, Over, and Down frame. What Flash does not do, however, is add a Hit state that defines the clickable area of the button. You'll have to add a keyframe on this state to make the button function. To do so, click in the empty cell of the Hit frame and choose Insert | Keyframe.

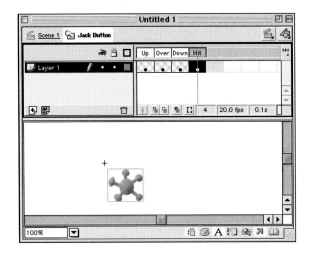

Import your Fireworks button frames into the new Flash button symbol.

4 Now you must reposition the three button states onto the center mark within the Symbol Editor window. Click to select the round button graphic in the Up state. As you drag, you will notice the rectangular bounding box, which contains a circle marking the object's center point. Place the circular center point of the object on top of the crosshairs, which mark the center of the symbol-editing window.

Repeat this step to center the Over, Down, and Hit states of the button. Your button is now complete.

5 Click on the Scene 1 link at the top left of the document window to return to the main movie stage.

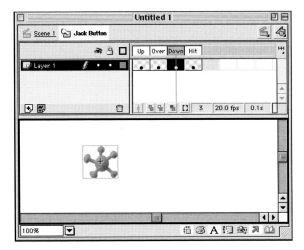

Center each of your button states on the crosshairs.

6 Now that you are back in the main movie area, choose Library from the Window menu. In the Library panel, you will see the three bitmap files that came in when you imported the Fireworks SWF file, along with the new Jack Button symbol you created.

Click and drag the Jack Button from the Library onto the document window (or the *stage* as it is sometimes called in Flash).

7 Save your file as **jackmovie01.fla**. Press F12 to preview your file in a browser. Once in the browser, when you mouse over the button, it should change to the Star Blob. Click it to see it squish.

Note: Previewing in a browser will not present you with as clean a result as you will get from your final exported movie.

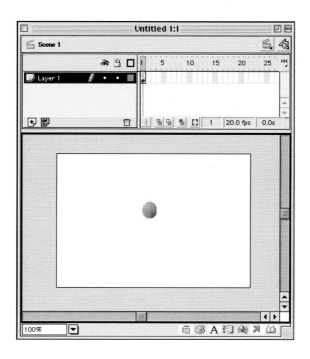

Drag the Jack Button symbol from the Library panel onto the main movie stage.

CREATING MOVIE CLIP FRAMES IN FIREWORKS

Currently, the Down state of your Flash button contains a single, static image—the splat you created. To liven up the design, you could replace the static image in the Down state with an animation, or movie clip. You can create the animation frames needed for the movie clip in Fireworks and then import the frames into Flash.

1 Go back to Fireworks and open **jack_movie _frames.png** from the **Project 7** folder on the accompanying CD-ROM. In the Frames panel, Option+click (or Alt+click) Frame 1 to create a duplicate on Frame 2.

For this project, you will create a total of five duplicate frames and will change the rotation of the jack object on each frame. This type of animation is called *frame-by-frame* animation because you alter each frame by hand.

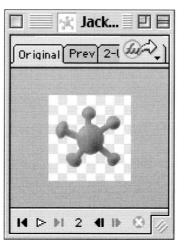

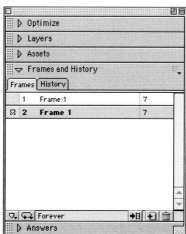

Duplicate Frame 1 and use the Transform tool to make changes on Frame 2.

99

2 Select the jack object on Frame 2 and choose Modify | Transform | Numeric Transform. In the Transform dialog box, select Rotate from the drop-down list and enter **72** in the field. Leave the Scale Attribute box checked and click OK.

3 Now duplicate Frame 2 to create Frame 3. Select and rotate the Frame 3's jack 72 degrees. Continue this procedure until you have a total of five frames that have each been rotated. Save your file as **jack_movie.png**.

4 Choose File | Export Preview. Be sure to use the same 32-bit PNG setting you used earlier and click the Export button. In the Export window, choose Macromedia Flash SWF from the Save As options. Click the Options button and select Maintain Appearance, **100%** JPEG Quality, All Frames, and a Frame Rate of **20**. Name the file **movie_frames.swf** and click Save. You can find the same file in the **Project 7** folder on the accompanying CD-ROM.

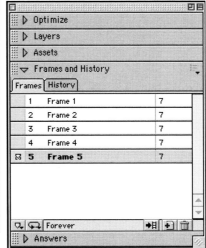

Create five duplicate frames and rotate the jack object on each frame by 72 degrees.

5 Switch back to Flash with your **jackmovie01.fla** file open. Open the Library panel by choosing Window | Library (if it is not already open). In the Library panel, click the Plus (+) sign icon to create a new symbol. Name the new symbol **Jumpin** and select the Movie Clip Behavior option. Click OK. The Movie Symbol Editor window opens automatically.

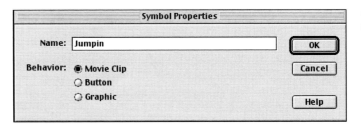

Create a new movie clip symbol called Jumpin.

6 Choose File | Import. In the Import window, locate your **movie_frames.swf** file or use the one in the **SWFs** folder in the **Project 7** folder on the accompanying CD-ROM.

On a Mac, select the file in the left pane and then click the Add button to move it to the right pane. Click the Import button. All five frames of your Fireworks movie will appear in the Timeline window.

In Windows, browse to and select **movie_frames.swf**.

To exit the movie clip editor, click on the Scene 1 link in the upper-left corner of the document. Notice that the Library panel now includes the imported graphics for the movie clip.

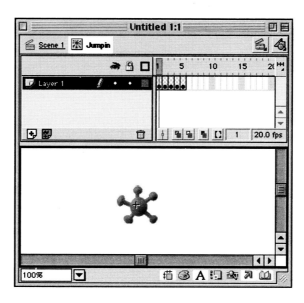

Import your Fireworks animation into the new Flash movie clip.

Note: To center the animation in the document, you will have to select each frame in the timeline and drag the graphic to the center crosshairs.

---

7 In the Library panel, double-click the Jack button to open the Button Symbol Editor window. Click on the Down state of the button and delete the Jack object. Drag the Jumpin movie clip from the Library panel into the center of Down state of the button. You have just replaced the static Down-state image with an animated one!

Click on the Scene 1 link to return to the main window.

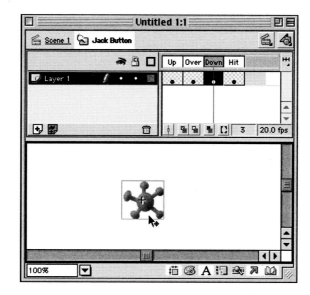

Replace the static image in the Down state with your new animated movie clip.

8 Press F12 to preview your file in the browser. Once in the browser, when you mouse over the button, it should change to the Star Blob. Click on it and your jack will twirl.

Preview your completed Flash button in a browser. Click on the button to see the animation.

MODIFICATIONS

Another way to move files from Fireworks to Flash is to simply copy and paste—no exporting, no saving, no nothing. If you use the normal copy function in Fireworks, in Flash you will paste a bitmap version of your objects, preserving their appearance. If you choose Fireworks's Copy Path Outlines function from the Window menu, you will preserve the vector status of your elements after they are pasted into Flash.

1 In Fireworks, open the **jumping_jack_logo.png** file from the **Project 7** folder on the accompanying CD-ROM. Select all the contents of the **gradient text** layer and choose Edit | Copy. (All other layers have been locked, so you can choose Edit | Select All.)

Note: Ray Larabie, whose site is at **www.larabiefonts.com**, designed the font I used for the **jumpin_jack_logo.png** file. He creates beautiful typefaces that he generously distributes to the World Wide Web community. He also sells some of his type designs and accepts donations online. Be sure to check out his wonderful work.

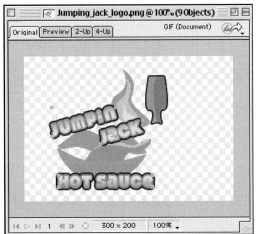

In Fireworks, select and copy all text elements of the **jumping_jack_logo.png** file.

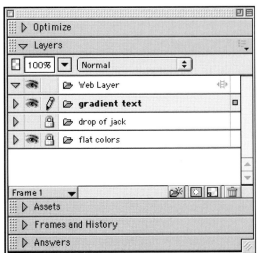

2 Go to Flash and open **jackmovie02.fla** from the **Project 7** folder on the accompanying CD-ROM. Rename Layer 1 with the button on it to **jack** by double-clicking the layer's name. Create a new layer by clicking on the Plus (+) sign icon in the lower right and name it **text**. Move the new **text** layer below the **jack** layer. With the new layer selected, choose Edit | Paste.

The text appears on the screen in all its gradient glory.

3 Create another new layer and name it **flat colors**. Make sure it is the bottommost layer in the movie.

4 Go back to Fireworks. Unlock the **flat colors** layer and lock the **gradient text** layer. Choose Edit | Select All to select all elements of the **flat colors** layer. Choose Edit | Copy Path Outlines.

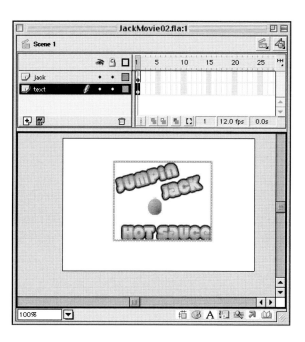

Paste elements from Fireworks directly into Flash.

5 Go to Flash, make sure the **flat colors** layer is selected, and paste! The vector status is retained in Flash, and you save on file size.

6 Save your file as **jackmovie_final** and test it in the browser by using the F12 key. When you click on the jack, it dances on the tip of the tongue.

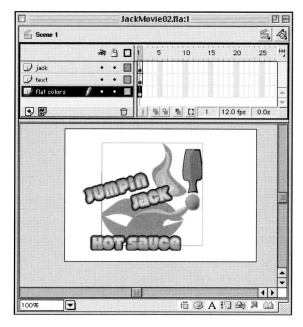

If you use Fireworks's Copy Path Outlines function, your artwork will remain as vectors in Flash.

LARGE-SCALE LINK MANAGEMENT

"Our personalities determine our destinies."

—LISA LOPUCK

Maintaining Link Consistency

When working with a team of people on a single web site project, the more resources you can share, the more you can streamline the production process and reduce duplicate efforts. In web design, it simply pays to be organized. Fireworks offers a number of collaborative workflow features, such as the URL panel and Find and Replace, that enable you to manage a large number of links across multiple pages to help a design team ensure consistency throughout a web site project.

Project 8

Large-Scale Link Management

by Lisa Lopuck

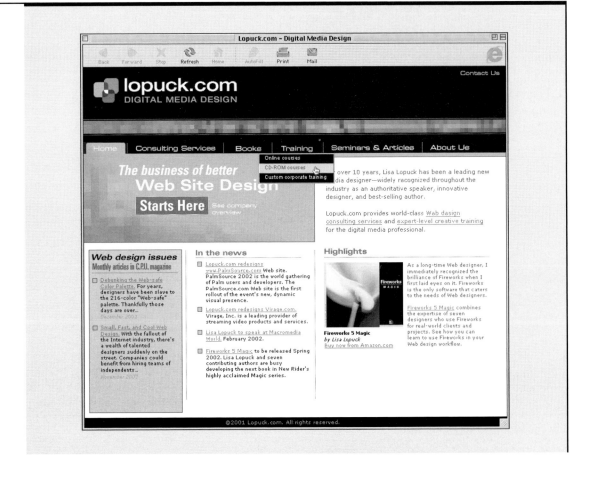

GETTING STARTED

For this project, the assumption is that you are working on a medium- to large-scale web site that has perhaps 50 links or so. When multiple people are working on a site of this size, it's important for everyone to use the same set of links when building out his portion of the site. The **Project 8** folder on the accompanying CD-ROM contains a "master list" of links that you will use to complete a few pages for Lopuck.com. Thanks for your help!

Using the URL Panel

The URL panel, located in the Windows menu, enables you to import an HTML file (that has links in it) to use as a list of links. The URL panel reads the HTML file and extracts all the HREF links it finds—conveniently listing them all in the panel. You can then apply these links to any hotspot or slice object in your Fireworks document. As you work, you might find that you need to add links to the list. The URL panel enables you to add, subtract, and modify links in the list and then export the final list for someone else on the team to use.

1 In Fireworks, open **lopuck_home.png** from the **Project 8** folder on the accompanying CD-ROM. When prompted, go ahead and change any fonts that are missing on your system. This home page has a number of hotspots, text links, and slices that need links applied to them.

2 From the Window menu, open the URL panel. Choose New URL Library from the options pull-down tab (in the upper-right corner). Name the new library **Lopuck.com** (after the name of the company) and click OK. In the URL panel, choose your newly formed library from the pull-down list—it might not be automatically selected in the list.

Now that you have a new URL library, you can start adding links to it for this project. Keep in mind that URL libraries are stored in the Fireworks Configurations folder, not with the document.

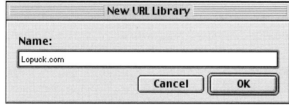

Name your new link library after the project you are working on.

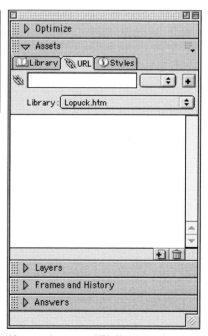

After creating a new URL library, it will appear in the pull-down menu.

3 In the URL panel, choose Import URLs from the options pull-down tab. Locate **lopuck_links.htm** in the **Project 8** folder on the accompanying CD-ROM and click OK. A list of 20 or so links will load into the URL panel.

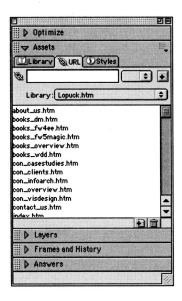

You can load any HTML document into the URL panel. Only the links will be displayed.

4 Turn on the **Web** layer's visibility in the Layers panel. Select the top-left slice covering the Lopuck.com logo. The logo will serve as a redundant quick link back to the home page. In the URL panel, select **index.htm** from the list.

That's it! You've just applied the **index.htm** link to the logo. Apply the **index.htm** link to the Home tab slice in this same manner.

5 Apply links to the remaining top-level navigation tabs:

■ For Consulting Services, use **con_overview.htm**.

■ For Books, use **books_overview.htm**.

■ For Training, use **train_overview.htm**.

■ For Seminars & Articles, use **semart_overview.htm**.

■ For About Us, use **about_us.htm**.

Select the Contact Us slice in the upper-right corner and apply **contact_us.htm**.

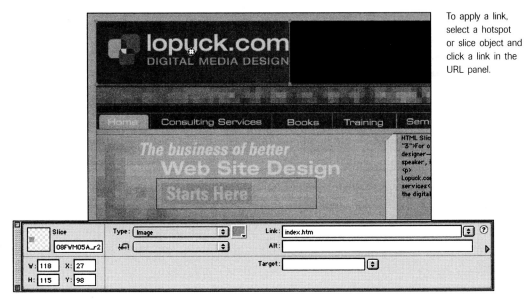

To apply a link, select a hotspot or slice object and click a link in the URL panel.

6 Select the Consulting Services tab. Notice that this tab has a pop-up menu associated with it. Double-click the outlined image of the pop-up menu to access the Editor window.

7 In the Pop-Up Menu Editor, click inside the Link field next to "Web site design overview." Select **con_overview.htm** from the drop-down menu in the Link field. Notice how all of the activated links from the URL panel are conveniently located in the Pop-Up Menu Editor window. Click Done after applying the link; you do not need to bother filling in the remaining links.

8 Click to select the top slice object over the "Web design issues" section of the page. This slice is a text slice, meaning it will export live HTML text as opposed to a bitmap graphic. In the Properties Inspector, click the HTML Edit button. The HREF for "Debunking the Web-Safe Color Palette" is currently blank, and there is no link in the URL panel for this particular article.

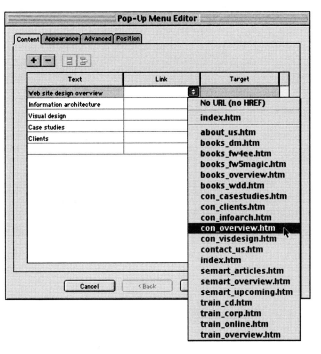

All of your imported links from the URL panel will show up in the Pop-Up Menu Editor window.

9 In the pop-up HTML Edit Slice window, replace the hash mark (#) in the link with **articles/dec2001.htm**. Select and copy the link so that you can add it to the URL panel in the next step. Click OK.

Now, when you export this page, the sliced region you edited will export as HTML code instead of as a graphic, and it will include your new link.

You can edit the HTML code of a text slice.

10 In the URL panel, paste the link into the link field and click the Plus (+) sign icon to add it to your list of links.

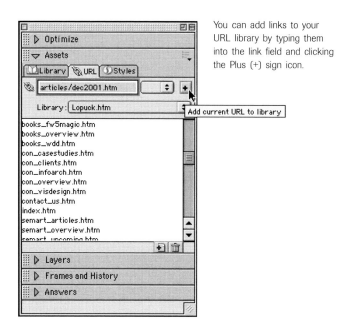

You can add links to your URL library by typing them into the link field and clicking the Plus (+) sign icon.

UPDATING AND EXPORTING LINK LIBRARIES

So far in this project, you've imported and applied links to various interactive elements. Where the URL panel really comes in handy, however, is for document-wide changes. The Lopuck.com home page features many redundant links. For example, both the logo and the Home tab share the same link. If you need to change the **index.htm** link to **index1.htm**, you can do so once in the URL panel. All objects that reference that link will automatically update.

1 Open **lopuck_home2.png** in Fireworks. Make sure nothing is selected in the document. In the URL panel, select **index.htm**. Choose Edit URL from the options pull-down tab. Change **index.htm** to read **index1.htm**. Check the Change All Occurrences in Document option and click OK.

Now, if you select the logo slice and the home tab slice, you'll see that they've been updated accordingly.

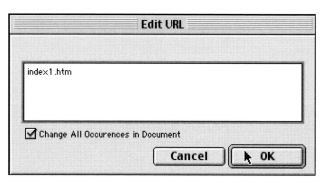

The URL panel enables you to instantly update all occurrences of a link within your document.

2 Select the hotspot covering the Starts Here button. Currently, this button links to the consulting overview page, but the button should actually link to a more general company overview. In the Properties Inspector, change the link to **lopuck_overview.htm** and press the Enter or Return key. In the URL panel, choose the Add Used URLs to Library option from the options pull-down tab.

3 To export your updated list of links, choose Export URLs from the options pull-down tab. Name the set **lopuck.com2.htm** and click Save.

Tip: If you have added unique links to your document or are working with a document that already has links that are not part of the library, the Add Used URLs to Library option is a quick way to augment your link list.

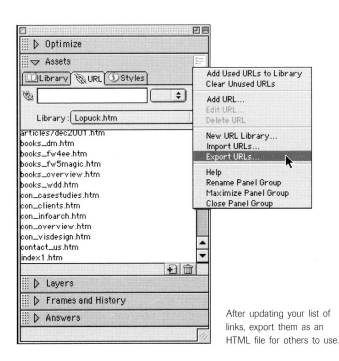

After updating your list of links, export them as an HTML file for others to use.

MODIFICATIONS

Unfortunately, the URL panel is capable of updating link usage only within a single document. If you have a number of documents for a site that all use the same set of links, updating links across all documents can pose a problem. The best way to update links across multiple documents is to use the Project Log and Find and Replace features. The Project Log enables you to target a specific set of project files (that are not necessarily in the same folder) so that the Find and Replace function can carry out a number of automated tasks on the set.

1 In Fireworks, open the Project Log from the Window menu. Click on the Options pull-down menu to add a few files to the Project Log for processing. Locate and import both **lopuck_sub1.png** and **lopuck_sub2.png** from the **Project 8** folder on the accompanying CD-ROM. Click the Done button to close the Project Log.

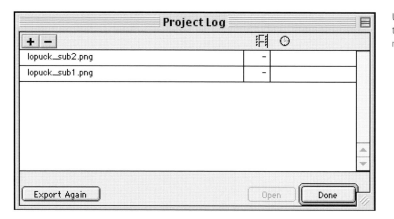

Use the Project Log to track the progress of changes made to multiple files.

2 Start a new document of any size. You only need this new document to access the Find and Replace window. Open the Find and Replace panel from the Window menu. From the top drop-down list, choose Search Project Log. In the second drop-down list, choose Find URL. In the Find field, enter **index.htm**—the old home link. In the Change To field, enter **index1.htm**. Click Replace All.

After a few minutes of chugging away, opening both the **lopuck_sub1.png** and **lopuck_sub2.png** files, Fireworks will tell you that four changes were made.

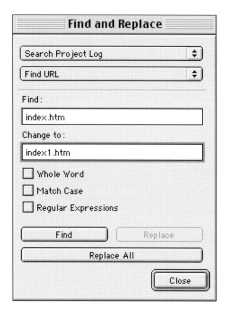

You can set the Find and Replace function to act on files in the Project Log.

3 Open the Project Log again from the Window menu. In the right column, you'll see the date and time stamp of your Find and Replace action. To verify that the changes took place, select **lopuck_sub1.png** and click the Open button. Select the slice over the logo and make sure it now reads **index1.htm** in the Properties Inspector.

Note: To preview the entire page in a browser, press F12.

Note: Many of this web site's links are embedded within the text slices. Fireworks's URL Find and Replace feature will not work on the text slices, but after you export the page and open it in Dreamweaver, you can use Dreamweaver's Find and Replace to update the links.

Open the subpage and test the links to verify that they were changed.

THE ULTIMATE
NAVIGATIONAL BAR

"When you get to the end of your

rope, tie a knot and hang on."

—FRANKLIN D. ROOSEVELT

BUILDING A WEB NAVIGATION BAR

Web site navigation is an important factor in

determining the quality of a user's experience.

Therefore, it's worth putting in the time to plan

out a visually compelling and easy-to-use

navigation system that's easily updated as the

site expands and evolves. Fireworks button

symbols not only make it easy to design a

great navigation system, they also give you the

flexibility you need to update your site painlessly.

The Ultimate Navigational Bar

by Joyce J. Evans

GETTING STARTED

In this project, you'll make a complete navigation system with just two button symbols. (Symbols are reusable art elements in Fireworks.) Though you will be working with two symbols, Fireworks enables you to make the necessary text and link changes to each copy of the symbols—enabling you to build a unique, multibutton navigation system. The other advantage of working with symbols is that if you make a graphical change, you instantly change all copies, or instances, of the symbol. In addition, if you build your symbols with vector tools, your navigation system will be completely scalable without compromising image quality. The final illustrations and all the source files needed to complete the project can be found in the **Project 9** folder on the accompanying CD-ROM. Project files that were saved after each section of the project, also are located in the folder, so you can jump in at any time.

MAKING THE BUTTON GRAPHICS

Any object—bitmap or vector—can be used as a button. In this first section, you will use the vector tools to make a background illustration for the button symbol so that it will remain fully editable.

1   In Fireworks, start a new file that is 250×75 pixels with a transparent background and 72dpi resolution. Select the Rectangle tool and draw a rectangle. In the Properties Inspector, change the size of the rectangle to 180×42, the Stroke to None, the Fill to Pattern, and select the Wood pattern. Save the file as **mybutton.png**.

2 In the Properties Inspector, click the Plus (+) sign icon to access the Effects list and choose Adjust Color | Hue and Saturation. Use the following settings:

Hue: **–13**

Saturation: **–55**

Lightness: **–25**

The wood pattern is now a darker shade. In the next step, you will begin to roughen up the wood to make it look older and more distressed (like driftwood).

3 Select the Reshape Area tool (located under the Freeform tool). In the Properties Inspector, enter a Size of **10** and a Strength of **80%**. Zoom in close, about 200%, so that you can see the edges you are going to alter. Begin to push in on all four edges to make them jagged. You might need to ungroup the image before you begin working.

4 When the edges look good to you, select the button, click the Plus (+) sign icon to access the Effects list, and choose Shadow and Glow | Drop Shadow. Use a Distance of 5 and a Softness of 3. Leave the Angle and Opacity settings at their defaults.

The Distance setting determines how far from the object the shadow will fall. You also can adjust the angle of the shadow if you'd like, ass well as the opacity.

5 Next add a couple of screws to the wood. Draw a small circle with the Ellipse tool. In the Properties Inspector, make the size of the circle 13×13 pixels and choose a Radial fill. Click the Fill color box to edit the gradient. Set the first color box to white and the box on the right to a dark gray.

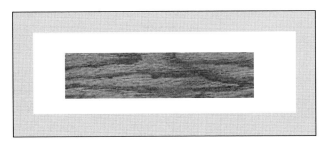

Apply a wood pattern fill to the button shape.

Use the Reshape Area tool to roughen the edges of the button.

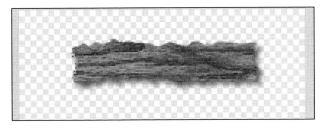

The drop shadow effect adds a bitmap look to the vector button shape.

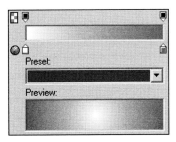

Apply a radial gradient fill to the circle screw shape.

6 With the Pointer tool, select the screw. Move the round gradient handle to the right to reposition the white spot so that it looks like a shine of light coming from the right.

7 To inset the screw, click the Plus (+) sign icon to access the Effects list in the Properties Inspector and choose Bevel and Emboss | Inset Emboss. Use a Width of 1, a Softness of 1, and an Angle of 135.

Use the gradient handles to position the white spot in the upper right of the screw.

8 To add the lines for the screw, use the Text tool to type an X. (I used Arial, 12 points.) Close the Text window. In the Properties Inspector, click the Plus (+) sign icon to access the Effects list and choose Bevel and Emboss | Inset Emboss with a Width of 1 and a Softness of 1. Group the circle and the X. Copy this first screw and place one on the right and one on the left near the top of the wood slat. Save your file.

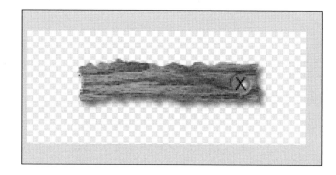

Use the Text tool to add an X to the screw.

Note: A copy of this button is saved as **button.png** in the **Project 9** folder on the accompanying CD-ROM.

MAKING THE BUTTON SYMBOLS WITH TEXT

Making button symbols in Fireworks can really speed up your workflow. A button symbol enables you to define all the button states (Up, Over, Down, and Over While Down) needed to make an interactive rollover element. You can make one button and then place as many instances of the same button into your document as you'd like. You can then modify individual button instances as needed, or you can change all of the instances at once by updating the original symbol.

1 Start a new document that is 200×75 pixels with a white canvas.

2 Choose Edit | Insert | New Button from the menu. Open your saved **mybutton.png** or the **button.png** file included in the **Project 9** folder on the accompanying CD-ROM. Choose Select | Select All and group the button with its screws. Copy the button and then paste it into the Up state of your Button Editor window. With the button selected, open the Window | Align panel, select the To Canvas option, and click Align Center Vertical and Center Horizontal (the two center icons of the Align portion of the Align panel).

3 Select the Text tool and click the button to add a text label. Type **Home** and then select the text with the Pointer tool. In the Properties Inspector, select the No Anti-Alias option and set the font to Georgia, the color to #6FA365 (a green shade), the size to 18, and the alignment to center. Click the Stroke Color Swatch icon and choose black.

The center alignment only centers the text in its own text box, not on the button. You can position the text by eye or use the Align panel. I find that I still adjust it just a bit. By center-aligning the text, when you make changes to each button instance, the text will always be centered.

4 Click the Over tab and click the Copy Up Graphic button to place a copy of your graphics in the Over state. Select the text, change the color to #D0BAAA, and remove the stroke.

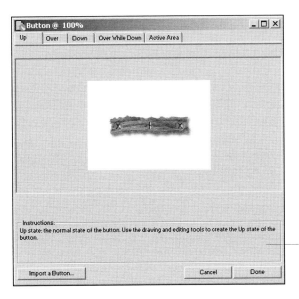

Paste your button illustration into the Up state of the Button Editor window.

The center-alignment setting ensures that your text will be centered on all instances of the button symbol.

Note: In Fireworks 4, if you added the text now, every time you changed the text on a symbol instance, a new symbol would be generated in the Library. This means that if you wanted to edit something like the button's color, you'd have to edit every symbol separately. In Fireworks MX, you can change the text of each instance without Fireworks generating multiple symbols.

Note: The text in this button is relatively large and easy to read, regardless of the antialias settings. If you use small text, however, you will get sharper results by using no antialias.

5 Click the Down tab and click the Copy Over Graphic button. Select the background graphic and, in the Properties Inspector, click the Plus (+) sign icon to access the Effects list. Choose Bevel and Emboss | Inset Emboss and use a setting of 2 for both the Width and the Softness. Click Done to close the Button Editor window and save the document as **home.png**.

When a user clicks your button, the Down state is what he will see. Because of the Inset Emboss effect applied, the button will look depressed.

Apply a bevel effect to the Down state graphic.

6 Make another button symbol (by choosing Edit | Insert | New Button) and repeat these steps but reverse the text colors. Make the button text "Products" with an Up state color of #D0BAAA and a black stroke. In the Over state, change the text color to bright green with no stroke.

A separate symbol is needed because of the new colors. If you edit the symbol, all instances with the tan text will change.

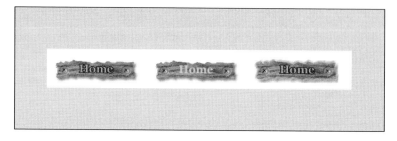

Both buttons should have three different states: Up, Over, and Down.

Note: A faster way to make the second symbol is to add text to the **home.png** file and resave it under a new name.

ASSEMBLING A NAVIGATION BAR

If you were to build a navigation bar in your document by adding multiple instances of one button symbol, and then change each instance in your workspace, Fireworks would turn each changed instance into a new symbol. (You'd see your Library panel fill up with a new symbol every time you made a change to an instance.) In this next section, you will build a fully editable, multibutton navigation bar as one button symbol. In effect, you will be embedding multiple symbols within a single new symbol.

1 Open the **tree.png** file from the **Project 9** folder on the accompanying CD-ROM.

2 Choose Edit | Insert | New Symbol from the menu and select the Graphic option. Drag the palm tree from the document into the Symbol Editor window.

3 Open the Library panel from the Window menu and choose Import Symbols from the Library Options pop-up menu. Navigate to the **Project 9** folder and import the **homebutton.png** file. In the Symbol Import window, select the symbol and import it. Repeat this process to import the symbol within the **productsbutton.png** file.

4 In the Layers panel, double-click Layer 1 (with the palm tree) and check the Share Across Frames option. Click outside of the mini pop-up window to close it.

Sharing the layer will put the tree graphic in each frame for the different states of the button.

5 In the Layers panel, add a new layer. (It will be called Layer 2.) Click Layer 2 to select it. Drag the two imported buttons from the Library panel into the Symbol Editor window, placing them on Layer 2.

Note: In Fireworks MX, by default, the Library panel is in the panel group area in the Assets category. Everything you make a symbol will show up in the Library panel. In step 5, you drag an instance (copy) of each symbol into the Symbol editor, which will embed a button symbol within your graphics symbol.

6 Select the Products button and, in the Properties Inspector, change the width of the button to **120**. Press Enter or Return. Select the Home button in the Symbol Editor window and choose Modify | Transform | Free Transform. Rotate about 45 degrees. Double-click to accept the transformation.

Drag the palm tree illustration into the Symbol Editor window.

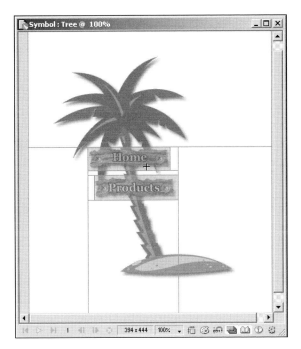

You can embed button symbols inside of the graphic symbols.

The width is being shortened on one button to add a more rustic and carefree look to the design. The rotation adds to the haphazard look.

7 Place the Home button at the top of the tree trunk, overlapping the leaves a bit. Place the Products button just below the Home button.

8 In the Properties Inspector, change the link of the Home button to read **index.html**. (Press the Return or Enter key after entering the new link.) Select the Products button and add the link **products.html**.

Note: While you are adding the links for the buttons, it's a good idea to get into the habit of adding Alt (alternative) text as well. The Alt text is what a user sees when she mouses over an image.

9 Drag another instance of the Home button into the Symbol editor and place it below the Products button. In the Properties Inspector, change the name from "Home" to "Services" and the link to **services.html**.

10 Drag another instance of the Products button into the Symbol Editor window. Place it below the Services button. In the Properties Inspector, change the text to "About Us" and its link to **aboutus.html**. Choose Modify | Transform | Free Transform and rotate the About Us button slightly. Drag an instance of the Home button into the Symbol editor. Change the name to "Contact Us", the link to **contactus.html**, and its width to **120**. Position this last link at the bottom of the tree trunk.

Use the Properties Inspector to change the text and links of button symbols.

The completed navigation bar should have five buttons named, linked, and placed in a horizontal row.

11 Close the Symbol Editor window and save the document as **mynavigationsymbol.png**. A copy of this navigation symbol is saved as **navigationsymbol.png** in the **Project 9** folder on the accompanying CD-ROM.

Now that you've built and saved your navigation symbol, you can import it into any document and voilá—have an instant navigation bar.

MODIFICATIONS

When you use symbols in Fireworks, making modifications is a breeze. Any changes you make to the original symbol will alter all instances of that symbol. In this project, you built a single navigation bar symbol out of just two button symbols. To alter the navigation bar, therefore, you must change one or both of the two button symbols.

1 Open **navigationsymbol.png**.

2 Open the Library panel and double-click the Home button symbol to edit it. (You must click the Home button image, not its name, to edit.)

3 In the Button editor, select the button and choose Modify | Ungroup. Now select and delete the two screws. Select the wood-like button graphic, open the Styles panel (Assets category of the panel group area), and click Style 16 in the lower-left corner of the window. Click Done to close the Button Editor window.

When you change the wood grain to the green grid and removed the screws, all the instances of the Home button symbol are changed at the same time. All the buttons with the green text used the Home button symbol.

When you make a change to a symbol, your changes will ripple through to all of its instances.

4 Double-click the Products button and ungroup the illustration. Again, delete the screws and select the underlying wood button graphic. In the Styles panel, choose Style 29. Click Done to close the Button Editor window.

That's it! You've instantly updated the look of your navigation bar symbol.

By changing the button symbols embedded within the navigation symbol, you instantly change its look and feel.

PERFECT POP-UP
MENUS

"The backbone of surprise is

fusing speed with secrecy."

—VON CLAUSEWITZ

BUILDING POP-UP NAVIGATION MENUS

Forget applets! You can build pop-up windows in Fireworks without writing a line of Java or JavaScript code. Pop-up menus are used to tuck away links that would otherwise consume valuable screen real estate. When a user rolls over the top-level link, a neatly organized window containing second-level links will appear, only to disappear again when the mouse moves to a new area. The menu's cell and text colors can be selected from the Fireworks web-safe palette, and you can even use Fireworks styles to give your link buttons some extra flair.

Perfect Pop-Up Menus

by Anne-Marie Yerks

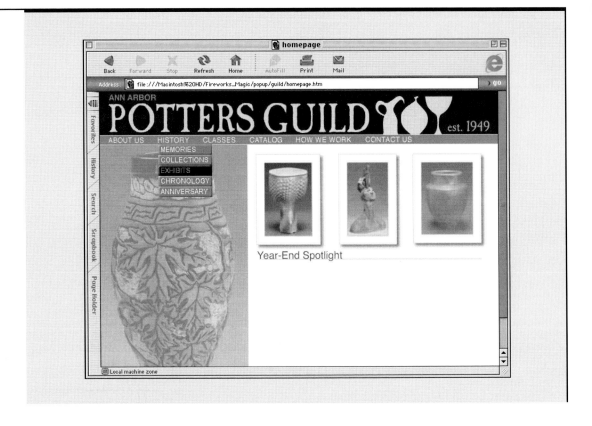

GETTING STARTED

Although pop-up menus are called pop-ups, you can designate any area inside the document for the window's placement. Therefore, your menus might appear below a link (as a drop-down menu) or to the side of a link. To build a pop-up menu, you create a hotspot or slice object and then assign the Insert Pop-Up Window behavior from the Behavior panel.

In this project, you'll use the **menu.png** file included in the **Project 10** folder on the accompanying CD-ROM to create a pop-up navigation bar for the Potters Guild site. This pop-up menu will be located beneath the site's banner image and will provide navigation to the lower-level pages.

After you create hotspots for the navigation buttons, you'll use the Insert Pop-Up Menu window to specify the options for the links and to set background cell and text colors. After creating the pop-up, you'll view the results inside a browser window.

CREATING A POP-UP MENU NAVIGATION BAR

Now you're ready to plunge into the world of pop-ups. Just go through the following steps to create a pop-up menu navigation bar using files provided on the accompanying CD-ROM. After you complete this exercise, you can apply these same technique to your own files.

1 Open the **menu.png** file from the **Project 10** folder on the accompanying CD-ROM. Save this file to your hard drive in a folder reserved for the exercises in this book.

This file contains a home page design for the Potters Guild web site. In the steps that follow, you will create a pop-up menu for each of the text links in the navigation bar. When these links are clicked in the final version, a pop-up window containing more links will appear beneath them.

2 Shift+select all six text links inside the navigation bar and choose Edit | Insert | Hotspot. Choose Multiple in the dialog box that appears. The link areas will highlight to indicate a series of hotspots. Deselect the hotspots by clicking away from them inside the canvas.

Each hotspot is an area marked by X and Y location coordinates in the HTML code. When you use Fireworks to create a hotspot, Fireworks automatically documents the coordinates when you export the HTML page. This way, you don't have to identify the coordinates on your own. Now that you've created a set of hotspots, you can assign the pop-up menu behavior to each of them.

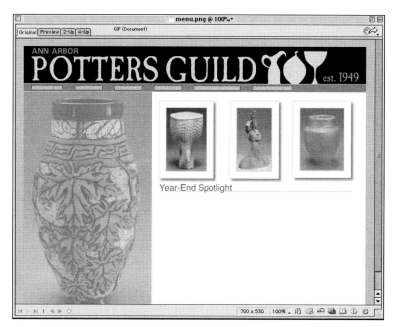

Hotspots will be marked with a highlighting color.

3 Now it's time to add the first set of pop-up menu items. Select the first hotspot, About Us. Open the Behaviors panel by choosing Window | Behaviors. Click the Plus (+) sign icon in the upper-left corner of the Behaviors panel to pull down the list of behaviors. Select Set Pop-Up Menu. The Pop-Up Menu Editor will appear. This window enables you to control all aspects of your pop-up menu.

Note: You also can apply the pop-up menu behavior to slice objects.

The Plus (+) sign and Minus (–) sign icons in the upper-left corner of the Behaviors panel enable you to assign the pop-up menu behavior to a selected hotspot or slice.

4 In the field labeled Text, enter the name of the first link you want to appear under the About Us menu. For this example, type **Members**. Press the Tab key to move your cursor into the Link field. Now enter the name of the HTML document to which the menu option should be linked, in this case **members.html**. Because you are not using frames and don't want the link to appear inside a new window, leave the Target field blank.

The list of links you build in the Pop-Up Menu Editor window will appear in this exact order when the user rolls over the About Us menu. Therefore, Members will be at the top of the menu.

5 When you add a menu item as you did in step 4, a blank row will appear beneath the first row. The new blank row is where you insert the data for the next item in the drop-down menu. Click inside the new row's Text field to type in the next link. Add **Founders** as your second item in this example. In the Link field, type **founders.html**. Click in the blank row beneath the Founders to add the next item.

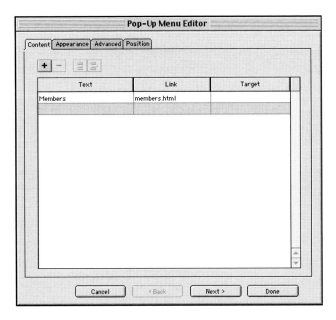

A new row will appear beneath the row in which you are currently adding data. Click inside the new row to add another menu item.

6 Add two more menu items to the About Us pop-up: **Teachers** and **Photos**. Make their links **teachers.html** and **photos.html**. When you've added all four menu items, click the Next button to move on.

7 In this next screen, you establish the pop-up menu's appearance. You can choose specific colors, fonts, and sizes for your menu items and for the background on which they appear. In many cases, you will want to adjust the settings in this area so that your pop-up menu compliments your page design. The first option in the Appearance tab enables you to specify whether you want to create your menu items with HTML or with images. For this exercise, click the radio button for the Image option.

The Image setting will generate graphics for the Up and Over states of the pop-up menu choices. This creates a more polished look, yet it might take longer to download. The HTML option will use colored table cells, not graphics, for the Up and Over states and will download very quickly.

Before moving on, make sure the pull-down menu to the right of Cells options is set to Vertical Menu, which indicates that the pop-up menu is formatted vertically rather than horizontally.

8 Next set the Font option to Verdana, Arial, Helvetica, sans-serif and set Size to 12. Do not select the bold or italic options. The text alignment should be set to left-aligned text.

This font and size match what was used for the menu's top-level links.

Note: Use the upward/downward-pointing Arrow icon that appears when you type in the Link field to enter URLs you have already typed. You also can use it to specify No URL.

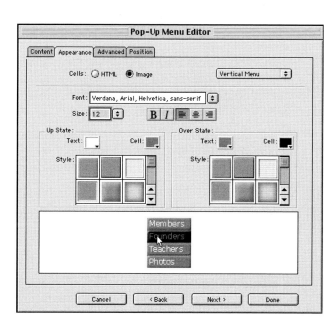

Establish the menu's appearance in the Appearance tab of the Pop-Up Menu Editor window.

9 The next step is to select colors for the text and background of your menu items. You will need to pick colors for the Up and Over states. The Up state is what the menu item will look like when it is not selected with the user's mouse. The Over state is what the item will look like when the mouse is hovering over it.

In the Up State section, click the text color chip and select white (#FFFFFF) from the color palette. Next click the Up State's Cell color chip. While the palette is open, you can move your cursor (which is now an eyedropper) over to your document and click to sample the gold color (#666633) of the navigation bar.

Note that a preview of your color choice appears in the area at the bottom of the window. This helps you visualize what the pop-up menu would look like and helps you create clash-free color schemes.

10 In the Over State section, set the text color to gold (#666633) and the Cell color to black (#000000).

11 Choose a graphical style for both the Up and Over states by clicking on one of the sample thumbnails. A plain beveled or embossed style is recommended because the added dimensional quality helps make each link clickable. Click Next to move on to the Advanced tab.

12 In the Advanced tab, you have the opportunity to control the way your menu items are spaced. The settings here are very similar to the HTML tags used to format tables and table cells. For this exercise, you only need to make two changes to the cell formatting. First you will change the Cell Width to 75 pixels, and then you will change the Cell Height to 20 pixels. To do this, click inside the Cell Width field and enter **75**. Then move over to the pull-down menu and choose Pixels. Do the same with the Cell Height. Leave the other settings as they are. You will be able to tweak them on your own after you have completed this exercise.

Basically, you are just rounding off the height and width of the cells to give the text a little more breathing room. If you were to leave the cells at the default setting, they would simply appear inside the menu at their default size.

Note: The Menu Delay setting can be used to create Help Tips to give users additional information about objects on the screen. To do this, use a three- or four-second delay setting instead of the Fireworks default.

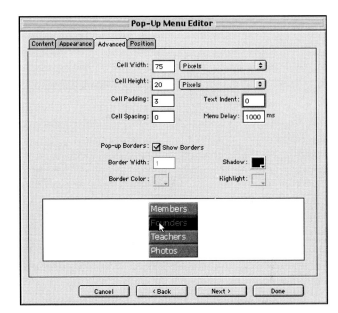

The Advanced tab enables you to format the spacing of the pop-up menu items.

13 Using the Position tab settings, you can indicate where on the screen you would like to place your pop-up menu. A series of four icons gives you general guidelines, but you can tweak the positioning by typing a specific coordinate inside the text field areas. For this exercise, click the first icon so that the menu will appear to the right of the hotspot. Because we are not working with a submenu, just leave that section of the dialog as is.

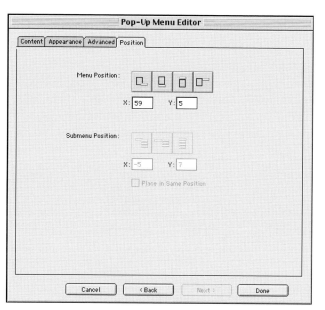

The Position tab is used to determine the placement of the pop-up menu in relation to its corresponding hotspot or slice.

14 Now you have finished the settings needed for this pop-up. Click Done to exit the Pop-Up Menu Editor.

Back in the document, a stack of outlined boxes is attached to the first hotspot, indicating the location of the pop-up menu. You can click and drag the outline to move its position if you so desire. A lasso-like line shows the menu outline attached to the hotspot. To make changes to the pop-up's content, simply double-click its outline.

Note: You cannot view your pop-up menus inside the Fireworks preview. Use the File | Preview in Browser option instead.

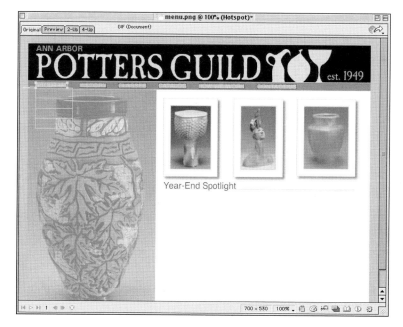

Click and drag the pop-up menu's outline to change its position. Double-click the outline to make changes to the menu item listing.

15 Now that you have completed the pop-up menu for the About Us section of the navigation bar, you can repeat the same steps to add pop-up menus to the remaining hotspots. Table 10.1 contains the data you will need for programming the pop-ups. If you don't want to build a pop-up for the remaining hotspots, you can open and examine the finished version in the **Project 10** folder. The completed file is called **menu_done.png**.

Nav bar Link	Pop-Up Menu Items	HTML Pages
History	Memories Collections Exhibits Chronology Anniversary	memories.html collections.html exhibits.html chronology.html anniversary.html
Classes	Registration Topics Resources Photos	registration.html topics.html resources.html photos.html
Catalog	By Member By Year By Keyword	member.php year.php keyword.php
How We Work	Point System Membership Glazes Kilns	points.html membership.html glazes.html kilns.html
Contact Us	None	None

16 The final step is to see how the pop-up menu will behave inside your web browser. Choose File | Preview in Browser and select your browser by name. When the file is opened inside the browser, roll over the buttons to test your pop-up menus.

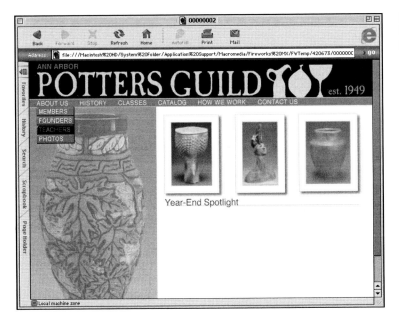

Choose File | Preview in Browser to see your pop-up menu in action.

EXPORTING POP-UP MENUS

In the preceding section, you created pop-up menus using hotspots rather than image slices. Therefore, the exporting process will involve use of a single image file (the page design) with the hotspot areas referred to inside the exported HTML code. Exporting the pop-ups in this manner is a little bit easier than it would be if you had used image slices. This is because you have fewer files to deal with.

1 Using the file you created in the preceding section (or the finished version **menu_done.png**), choose File | Export. In the Export dialog box, choose the folder into which you would like to save the page design image and the HTML file. In the Name field, type a filename with an .html or .htm extension. In the Save As drop-down list, choose HTML and Images. In the HTML drop-down list, choose Export HTML File. Click Save to save the files and exit the dialog box.

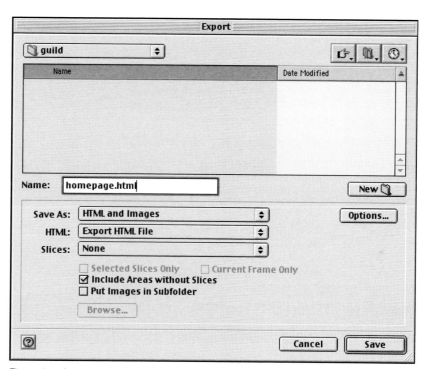

The settings for your pop-up menu export can be established in the Export dialog box.

2 Now you will take a look at the set of files that Fireworks just created. Choose File | Open and locate the folder containing your exported HTML and graphic files. Change the setting from All Readable Files to All Files. You should see a single HTML file, a set of GIF files for the pop-up menu buttons, and a single image file that is the page design.

In this list, you also should see a file with a .js extension. This is the JavaScript used for your pop-up menus. Aren't you glad you didn't have to write that on your own? Remember that the HTML and JS files must always be in the same folder (unless you update the JS file's path location in the HTML code). Click Cancel when you have finished examining this set of files. Don't forget to upload this file along with the rest to your web server when you publish your page.

3 Because you have now created an HTML file and a JS file, you should be able to view the results independently of Fireworks. Open your web browser. Choose File | Open and browse for the HTML file you created in step 2. Check to make sure your pop-up menus are working. If they are, you have successfully created a page containing pop-ups. Congratulations!

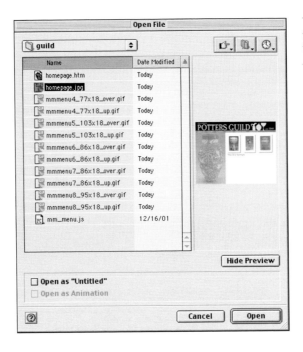

The set of files created by the export includes image files, an HTML file, and a JS (JavaScript) file.

MODIFICATIONS

By default, Fireworks uses the onMouseOver event handler in pop-up menus. This means that the menu appears when the user rolls over, or mouses over, the hotspot or image slice to which the menu is assigned. You can, however, change the event handler so that the menu appears when the hotspot or slice is clicked.

1 Select the hotspot or slice and open the Behaviors panel (Window | Behaviors). In the panel, click the Show Popup Menu action so that it is highlighted.

2 Click the down-pointing arrow located between the Events and Actions panes. From the context menu, choose onClick. This action makes it so that the user has to click on the button to see the pop-up menu.

> **Note:** You also can set the event handler so that the menu appears onMouseOut (when the mouse moves away from the designated area) or onLoad (when the page loads into the browser).

Change the event handler by clicking the down-pointing arrow located between the Events and Actions panes.

BONUS MODIFICATION: USING POP-UPS INSTEAD OF SWAP ROLLOVERS

Your pop-up menu doesn't have to contain multiple items. You can use it for a single item and can place it anywhere on the screen. For example, you can use a pop-up menu to reveal the artist's name when the user mouses over an image in the Potters Guild home page. When the link is clicked, the spotlight page opens in a new window. Although this type of interaction also could be accomplished with the Swap Image behavior, there is no reason why an HTML pop-up menu couldn't be used instead. By using a pop-up menu, you can cut down on your use of graphics and therefore increase your page's download performance. Pop-ups also make more efficient use of space because they are drawn on top of your interface (using cascading style sheet layers). The following steps show you how to do this.

1 Open the **menu.png** file from the accompanying CD-ROM. Select the first thumbnail image on the page (the textured red vessel) and choose Edit | Insert | Hotspot. In the Behavior panel, click the Plus (+) sign icon and choose Set Pop-Up Menu from the list.

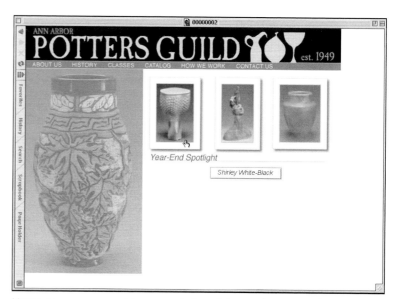

Moving the mouse over each image reveals the artist's name beneath the "Spotlight" sub head.

2 In the Pop-Up Menu Editor, add the name **Shirley White-Black** as the artist in the Text field. Enter **spotlight.html** into the Link field and click the Next button.

3 Under the Appearance tab, click the HTML radio button to indicate that you want the pop-up to use HTML rather than images. Set the pull-down menu to the Vertical Menu option. Set your Font and Size choices. In the bottom section, set your text and background color schemes. When you arrive at something you're satisfied with, click the Done button.

Though the rollover has a link, you are using it for informational purposes only—to display the artist's name. Because users will not be clicking on the rollover, it does not need to look clickable (by adding an emboss effect). You can choose any design you like.

4 In your document, click the hotspot to select it. Notice the blue outline below that indicates the pop-up menu. Click and drag the menu's outline and position it below the "Year-End Spotlight" text.

The blue outline indicates where the pop-up will appear after the page is published.

5 Choose File | Preview in Browser to see the results or open the **menu_done.png** file (from the accompanying CD-ROM) inside your web browser to see how all three thumbnails look when programmed with pop-ups.

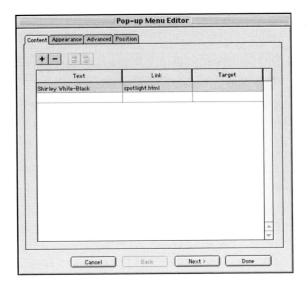

Enter the artist's name in the Text field and spotlight.html in the Link field.

TO DREAMWEAVER
AND BACK

"There is an empty space inside, waiting to

be filled with answers."

—STEVEN GROSVENOR

WORKING SMARTLY BETWEEN DREAMWEAVER AND FIREWORKS

What never ceases to amaze me is that even

though Dreamweaver and Fireworks have a

number of integrated tools and features

designed to drastically reduce development

time, people rarely use them. By understanding

how to use the round-trip features of these

two products, you can significantly streamline

your web design workflow.

Project 11

To Dreamweaver and Back

Steven Grosvenor

GETTING STARTED

The interface you see on this page was created entirely in Fireworks and Dreamweaver. Not only can you create crisp web interfaces in Fireworks, you also can "round trip" the graphics and HTML code created between Dreamweaver and Fireworks. This project will take you through the steps and potential pitfalls of exporting your Fireworks creations into a variety of different formats for use within your authoring environment and back into Fireworks for editing. All of the graphics and HTML source files needed to complete this project can be found in the **Project 11** folder on the accompanying CD-ROM.

You will learn how to slice graphics, attaching extended behaviors and URLs and working smartly to export the graphics you have created within Fireworks into Dreamweaver. You also will be shown how to make HTML changes and import those changes back into Fireworks for the full round-trip experience.

SLICING THE INTERFACE AND ASSIGNING BEHAVIORS

By slicing the interface and attaching behaviors, URLs, and image maps within Fireworks, you can effectively remove most of the coding required to gain interface functionality within the HTML authoring environment. By using Fireworks as your initial layout environment, you can maintain pixel-perfect control over how the design will look in the authoring environment and later in the live deployment environment.

1   Open the **webinterface.png** file from the **Project 11** folder on the accompanying CD-ROM.

2   Click the Eye icon next to the **Guides** layer in the Layers panel to show this layer. Using this layer as a visual guide, select the Slice tool and create a series of slices, splitting the interface into logical pieces. When you have finished slicing the interface, click the Eye icon again to hide the guides. Change the slice that is just below the "Download the User Guide" text from image to HTML. Click Edit within the Properties Inspector and enter this HTML snippet into the edit box:

```
<p>
<font size="1" face="Verdana, Arial, Helvetica,
sans-serif">
Click above to download the user guide
</font>
</p>
```

> **Note:** These steps were performed on a PC. If you use a Mac, when converting the image to HTML, you might need to select a text option, not HTML.

> **Note:** Extensively changing the code produced by Fireworks MX—for example, by adding form validation within Dreamweaver MX—will not be maintained in the round-trip environment and will be overwritten when the exported items are imported back into Fireworks.

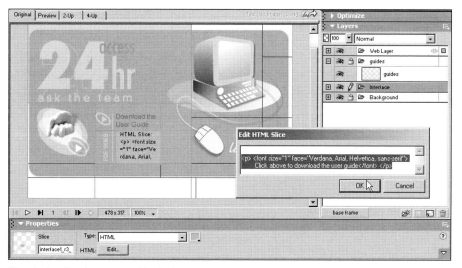

Slice the interface into manageable chunks.

> **Tip:** It can be more beneficial and controllable to format text within Dreamweaver MX using external style sheets rather than hard-coding font parameters within Fireworks. To do this, simply type the text that you want to appear into the HTML slice within Fireworks MX and export it to Dreamweaver MX. Within Dreamweaver, after opening the file, select the cell containing the text. Applying a CSS style from either an internal or external CSS file from within the CSS panel yields the same results as hard-coded formatting, but it gives you more flexibility.

3 Select the slice that is positioned above the mouse image and the Login icon. Then grab the Target icon that appears in the middle of the slice and drag it to the slice below. Doing so will create a swap image rollover. In the window that appears, click the More Options button.

From the dialog box, make sure the image has been swapped to the General MouseOvers (2) frame. Select the preload option and click OK.

> **Note:** If you accidentally create a swap image behavior that is not correct, you can delete it by moving your mouse over the line connecting the slice object to the destination slice (whereby it will change to a hand with small stop sign) and by clicking the line to remove the behavior.

4 Repeat these steps to create swap image rollovers for the slices located at the bottom-left corner.

If you preview the interface now, you'll see that when you mouse over the Go icon, an informational section appears at the bottom of the interface. Save your active document to a local drive.

5 Select the slice over the Help icon in the top right of the interface. Open the URL panel if it's not already open (Alt+Shift+F10). Select Import URLs from the Options pull-down menu and locate the **workflow.htm** file from the **Project 11** Folder on the accompanying CD-ROM. Click Import.

> **Note:** When creating slices or image maps, always try to think about how the design will look when exported as a Fireworks table or a series of CSS layers within Dreamweaver, especially if you are going to make significant changes to the cells or layers of your exported design.

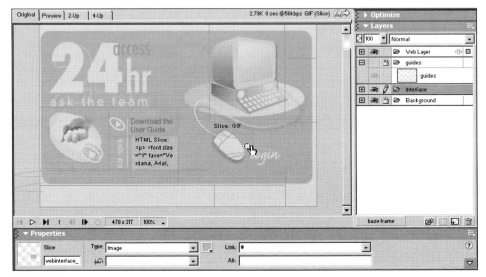

Attaching behaviors to the interface.

6 With the Help slice selected, click the **help.html** URL in the URL panel. Make the target _blank. Making sure the slice is selected, repeat steps 3 and 4 for this slice, assigning the mouseover frame to be **helpmouseovers**.

7 With the Login slice selected, click the **login.asp** URL in the URL panel, assigning a _blank target.

8 Now select the Download slice that contains the "Download the User Guide" text. Create a swap image rollover with the slice to the left and click the **download.html** URL in the URL panel.

If you preview the interface, moving the mouse over the relevant areas creates multiple disjointed rollovers within the preview image. Once again, save the active document to a destination of your choice.

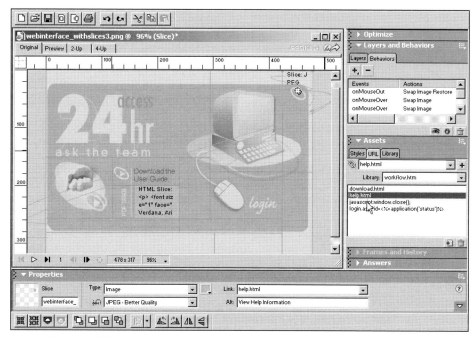

Attach behaviors and URLS to each slice in the interface.

EXPORTING THE INTERFACE TO DREAMWEAVER MX AS HTML

Now that you have attached the behaviors and URLs to the interface, it is time to export the page to an authoring environment for testing and alterations. The behaviors that Fireworks MX creates are editable within Dreamweaver MX. *Most* changes that you make within Dreamweaver MX will be preserved when you launch and edit the file in Fireworks again. For example, if in Dreamweaver MX you drastically change the table structure or add custom behaviors, your changes might be overwritten when you switch back to Fireworks MX. In this section, you'll export your interactive page into Dreamweaver MX for changes.

1 Open Dreamweaver MX. To export the interface, you need to define a site in Dreamweaver to hold and export the Fireworks HTML data. From Dreamweaver, choose Site | New Site. Select the Local Info tab within the Site Definition dialog box. Enter the site name and local root folder on your computer that you want the site to reside in.

2 Back in Fireworks, choose File | Export (Ctrl+Shift+R). You are presented with a list of export options. Due to the complexity of the interface, choose the following options:

File Name: webinterface.htm

Save as Type: HTML and Images

HTML: Export HTML File

Slices: Export Slices

3 While still in the Export window, click the Options button. Select the General tab and make sure that HTML style is set to Dreamweaver HTML. Click OK to return to the Export window. Navigate to the folder you selected as your Dreamweaver site folder and click Save.

4 Now let's export this design again, this time as a Dreamweaver Library Item rather than as HTML and Images. On your computer, find the folder you are using as your Dreamweaver site folder. Add a folder to this directory called **Library**.

Note: Ensure Fireworks MX is the primary editor for Fireworks PNG files within Dreamweaver by choosing Edit | Preferences. Then choose File Types | Editors from the selection list and assign Fireworks MX as the primary editor for PNG files. When you select graphics for editing, Dreamweaver will know to open Fireworks as opposed to a different graphic editor.

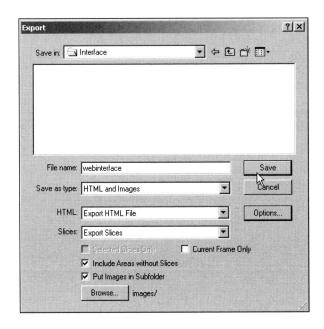

Export your Fireworks design to the Dreamweaver site folder.

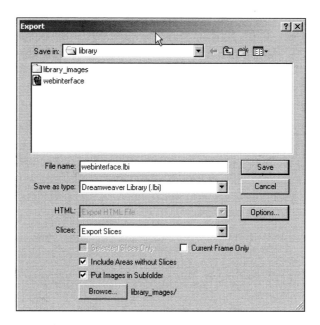

5 In Fireworks, choose File | Export and navigate to your new Library folder. Choose Dreamweaver Library (.lbi) from the Save As options. Name the file **webinterface.lbi** and click Save.

If you plan to use an element multiple times throughout the web site, saving it as a Library item enables you to update it once to automatically update all occurrences of it.

Export your Fireworks design as a Dreamweaver Library item.

ROUND-TRIP EDITING

Now that you've exported the page from Fireworks as both a normal HTML file and a Dreamweaver Library item, you can open them in Dreamweaver and make changes. In this section, you'll open the HTML file in Dreamweaver, make changes to it, and then switch back to Fireworks to see how your changes have been retained. While in Fireworks, you'll update the graphics and then switch back to Dreamweaver again.

1 Within Dreamweaver, open the **webinterface.htm** file that you exported from Fireworks. (Alternatively, you can copy the sample site structure from the **Project 11** folder on the accompanying CD-ROM to your locally defined site within Dreamweaver.)

2 Select the cell that contains the text slice that was created in Fireworks and set the background color to #ff6600.

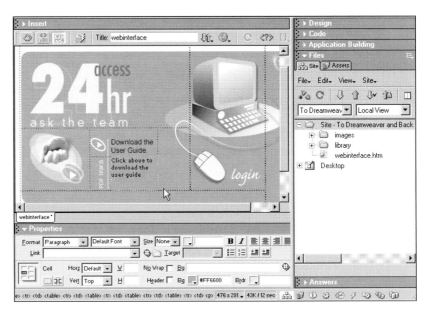

Making table formatting changes to the exported Fireworks HTML.

3 Select the table. To do so, click a graphic. At the bottom left of the document window, you'll see the HTML tag for the graphic. Click the <table> tag to select the table. In the Properties Inspector, click the down arrow in the bottom right to show advanced options and click the Edit button to open the table in Fireworks.

Dreamweaver opens the original PNG source file in Fireworks for editing. Fireworks retains the changes you made in Dreamweaver.

4 In Fireworks, open the Library panel. From the Options pull-down menu, select Import Symbols. Locate the **closewindow.png** file from the **Project 11** folder on the accompanying CD-ROM. In the Symbol Import window, highlight the close_window_up and close_window_down symbols and click Import. The symbols will appear in the Library panel.

Fireworks retaining code changes made within Dreamweaver.

5 Drag the close_window_up symbol from the Library panel and place it to the left of the Help icon within the base frame. Repeat for the close_window_down symbol, placing into the general mouseovers frame. Add a new slice for the Close Window graphic and alter the size of the surrounding slices. Now, with the slice selected, click the Compass icon in the center of the slice and select Add Simple Rollover Behavior behaviors;applying to slices;rollovers for this slice. Each icon should have its own slice.

6 In the Assets Panel | URL, add the URL **javascript:window.close();**.

Select the slice over the Close Window graphic and assign the JavaScript URL to it. Instead of a normal HTML link, you can force Fireworks to export a raw JavaScript command, which in this case will force the window to close.

Click the Done button at the top of the document to return to Dreamweaver with your new changes.

7 Back in Dreamweaver, you see the new table structure along with the new JavaScript command. To test the design, choose File | Preview in Browser.

Tip: Although Fireworks has a limited set of premade behaviors, you can type your own JavaScript commands into the URL panel. These commands, however, must be ones that can execute from within the HTML—without requiring setup in the Head section of the HTML document. It is useful to create a URL Library of your own commands for such purposes.

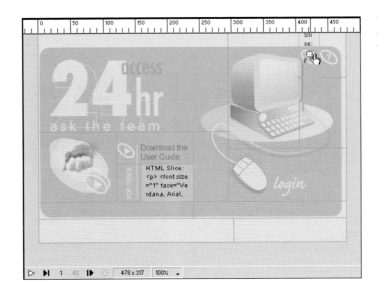

The new symbol and slice added to the interface within Fireworks.

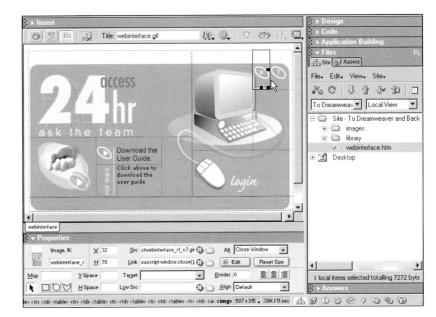

The interface now shows additional elements and behaviors within Dreamweaver.

MODIFICATIONS

Because Fireworks is not an HTML editor, it has a limited set of behaviors. Dreamweaver, on the other hand, offers a lot more interactive control over a web page. Fireworks, therefore, will not recognize many of the custom Dreamweaver behaviors you might add during the round-trip process and instead will overwrite them. In addition, Fireworks also has trouble rendering complex tables or nested tables that you create in Dreamweaver. To counteract these limitations, it's better to prepare and export each section of your Fireworks document separately and use Dreamweaver to assemble each component into a page.

1 In Fireworks, open the **webinterface_final.png** file included in the **Project 11** folder on the accompanying CD-ROM. Use the Crop tool to crop the document down to the size of one of the slices. Save the document with a new name. (Choose a name that describes the particular slice.)

2 Use the History panel to undo your steps so that you have the original layout again. Use the Crop tool again to crop the document to another slice. Save the file with a new name that describes that slice. Repeat this step until you have a number of separately saved files—one for each slice.

3 Open all of the individual PNG files. One by one, export each document as HTML and Images.

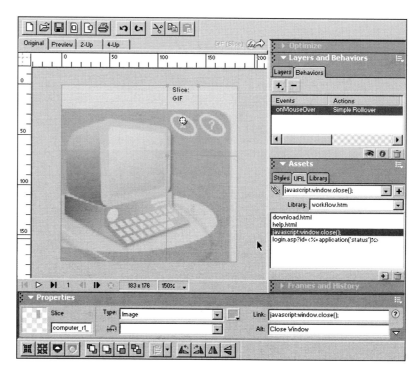

Cropping the interface to export individual items as Library items.

4 In Dreamweaver, open one of the exported HTML files. Select the table or image by clicking on a graphic. At the bottom left of the document window, you'll see the HTML tag for the graphic. Click on the <table> tag or <img> tag to select the table or the image depending upon whether or not the exported graphic contains more than one slice. Open the Assets | Library panel and click the Plus (+) sign icon to add the file to the Library. Name the new Library item accordingly and then close the HTML file. Repeat this for the remaining HTML files.

5 Create a new page in Dreamweaver. With the Table object, create a new table that has three columns and two rows, 100% width, and no border.

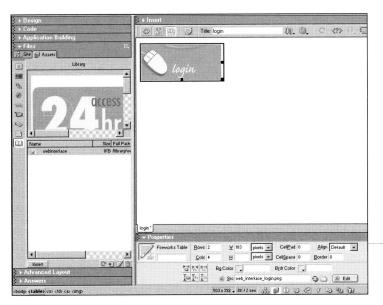

Building the interface from a series of Library items within Dreamweaver.

6 Drag and drop each library item into a separate cell in your new table. To re-create the Fireworks layout accurately, you might have to open the original design in Fireworks to use as a visual guide.

The end result is a series of Library items nested within the main table.

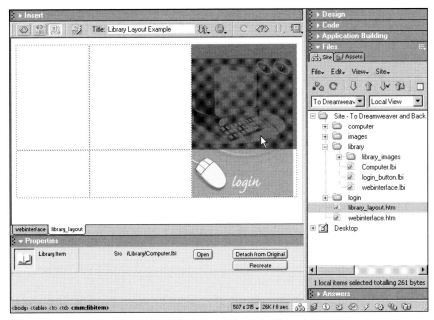

The interface is now being created from the exported Fireworks Library items.

7 To make a change to one of the Library items, double-click it. The Library item will open in a new window. Click the Edit button in the Properties Inspector to launch the original PNG file in Fireworks for changes. In Fireworks, try making a simple graphical change (such as adding text) and click the Done button to return to Dreamweaver.

Back in Dreamweaver, you'll see the Library item updated in the layout. Because each element of the layout is a separate file, making changes to one does not affect the others. This approach reduces the risk of overwriting important code associated with one of the other Library items.

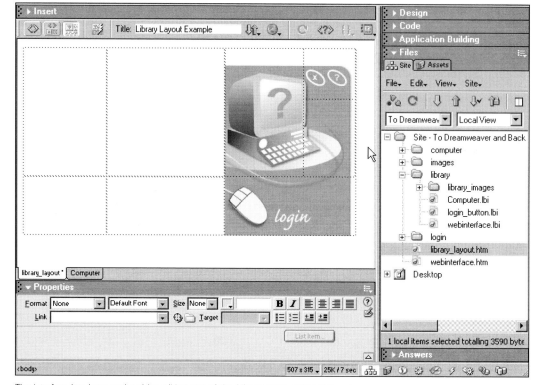

The interface has been updated by editing one of the Library items within Fireworks.

INSTANTLY UPDATED
WEB SITES

"Invisible thread emanating from her

fingertips spun together an entirely new

concept of time."

—HARUKI MURAKAMI, *SOUTH OF THE*
BORDER, WEST OF THE SUN

UPDATING WEB SITE GRAPHICS WITH BATCH PROCESSING TOOLS

When you are the one making site-wide

changes to a web site, the issue of web site

evolution takes on a whole different set of

meanings. You can't just open up Dreamweaver

and tell it to change the nav bar graphics to a

different shade of blue throughout every page

of the site. Though there is no easy answer to

such site-wide changes, Fireworks does offer

several automated features to make your life

a little easier.

Project 12

Instantly Updated Web Sites

by Jeffrey Bardzell

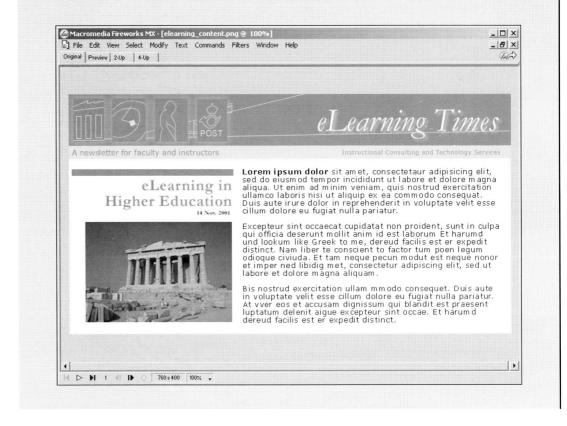

GETTING STARTED

In this project, you will work with one Fireworks page design that has been used to create a multipage HTML newsletter. This quarterly newsletter is ready for its next release, incorporating some user feedback that was collected during the last issue. In addition, the developers want to change the color combination to distinguish the two issues of the newsletter. To accomplish these changes without altering any of the already-exported HTML code, you'll use the Project Log in conjunction with the Find and Replace feature.

Note: Please refer to the CD-ROM for full-color versions of the project files.

The following is a list of the design changes that need to be addressed to complete the next version of the newsletter:

- The entire color scheme needs to be changed.

- Change the rollover icons' second frames to black and white. (They are currently in color.)

- Change Garamond to Times New Roman in the masthead and page-title graphics.

- The large photograph on each page was deemed too large; it needs to be resized down.

Note: To complete this project, you will need to use files from the **Project 12** folder of the CD-ROM. Specifically, you will be asked to use the **elearning_content.png** and the **pageheader.png** files.

USING FIND AND REPLACE WITH THE PROJECT LOG

The process of going from vector to bitmap to HTML can create some sizable inefficiencies. To compensate, Fireworks offers some productivity-enhancing tools like Find and Replace and the Project Log. The Project Log enables you to automate changes across a series of files and then re-export them with the same names. The Find and Replace function enables you to search for text, colors, and links across a document (or a series of files in the Project Log) and instantly update them. In this first section, you'll do a comparatively easy task: You will replace all of the Garamond text with Times New Roman.

1 With Fireworks and any file open (it doesn't matter which one), choose Edit | Find and Replace to open the Find and Replace panel.

2 In the first drop-down menu on the Find and Replace panel, choose Search Files from the list of choices. The Open File window appears.

The utility of Find and Replace is enhanced by the different source options. Though you will often use the default, Search Document, don't forget that you can simultaneously search multiple files.

3 Navigate to the **insidepages** folder in the **Project 12** folder and Shift+select to choose both of the PNG files in that folder: **elearning_content.png** and **pageheader.png**. Click Done.

The Find and Replace panel.

4 Back in the Find and Replace panel, choose Find Font from the second drop-down menu. After you select the Find Font option, the options below it will change, enabling you to select fonts.

5 Select Garamond from the drop-down list (below Find Font) and leave the Any Style and Min and Max default settings.

The reason you shouldn't change any of the other settings is that you are replacing all instances of Garamond, regardless of attributes such as size, style, and so on. Use these settings only if you want to further limit the Find and Replace operation.

> **Note:** If you do not have the Garamond font on your system, you will need to open the **elearning_content.png** file from the **Project 12** folder and, when prompted, change the font to one you have on your system. Do not use Verdana or Times New Roman because you will be changing to those fonts in this section.

6 In the lower section of the panel is the font Change To area. In that area, set the font to Times New Roman and leave the remaining options at their defaults.

7 Click the Replace All button. Fireworks automatically opens each of the files, makes the appropriate changes, and then closes them. Click the Close button. When finished, you will see a "search complete" message. Click OK to continue working.

8 Open both the **elearning_content.png** and **pageheader.png** files in the **Project 12** folder and verify that the font changes were made.

You'll notice that the eLearning Times title on the main page file now runs off the page. As you can see, the Find and Replace feature is not foolproof. Select and reposition the text or double-click the text and resize it.

Select the font that you'd like to change.

USING THE PROJECT LOG

In the preceding section, you saw that after you entered your parameters in the Find and Replace dialog box, Fireworks zipped right through and made all the changes. Of course, the changes were made inside Fireworks, and your HTML pages look the same as they did when you started. In this section, you'll use the Project Log to update those pages without even touching your HTML.

1 Open Window | Project Log from the Window menu.

The Project Log should have five entries in it. Each entry reflects the font Find and Replace function you performed earlier.

2 Hold down the Shift key and click to select the **elearning_content.png** and **pageheader.png** files.

It doesn't matter which of the **pageheader.png** files you choose because each listing represents a change in one of the pageheader's frames.

3 Click Export Again from the Project Log pop-up options menu.

4 In the Export window, the export settings for the pageheader document should appear because it was first in the Project Log list.

The default export setting for **pageheader.png** is Frames to Files, and to save each image as a GIF. Frames to Files exports each frame as an independent file, which is exactly how you want these four page header images. (It also proves that Fireworks really remembers each file's own export settings.) Click Save and choose Yes to the warning pop-ups that appear.

Note: One of the Export settings that Fireworks remembers is the path. Unfortunately, the path on my system when I created these files is probably not the same path as the one on your system. Be sure during this step that you navigate and save the files in the **insidepages** project folder.

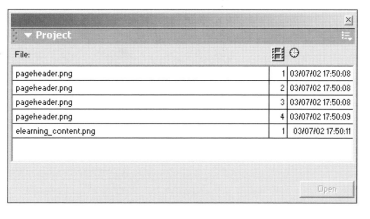

The Project Log lists all files affected by a Find and Replace operation that were not open at the time it was run.

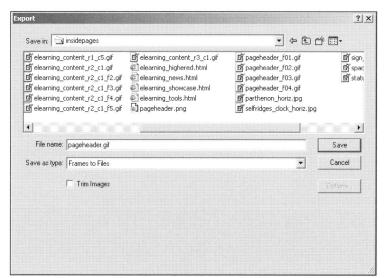

When you export using the Project Log, it remembers the original export settings so that you don't need to change them each time.

5 Click Save. A couple of pop-up warnings later (click on Yes for each warning) your images are updated. Immediately, another Export dialog box appears. This one is for **elearning_content.png**. For this file, you want the images but not the HTML re-exported. You also want Fireworks to export the slices so that they will appear updated in the HTML file.

6 Open your HTML files in a browser or HTML editor such as Dreamweaver. The fonts have indeed changed to Times New Roman, and you did it quickly with the help of Fireworks's Find and Replace feature.

Thanks to the Fireworks Find and Replace feature, the graphics have been quickly updated with the new font.

CHANGING THE COLOR SCHEME

Now that you have some experience with how the Find and Replace and Project Log features work, it's time to get down to business. In this section, you'll change the whole color scheme of the main page and its components. Though you will be changing only two files, the steps are identical to modifying any number of files.

Note: If you design your pages to be modular—that is, if you design a complete page in Fireworks and then spin off each of its main components into its own PNG file (Portable Network Graphic, which is Fireworks's native file format)—you will achieve significant productivity gains.

1 With Fireworks and at least the **elearning_content
.png** file open, select Window | Project Log to open
the Project Log again.

2 From the Options menu in the upper-right coner of
the Project Log, choose Clear All. For the verifica-
tion message that appears, click OK.

Files in the Project Log can stick around for several
sessions. When I am about to make any changes, I
clear it just to be tidy.

3 From the Project Log's option menu, choose Add
Files to Log. In the Open window, navigate to
and select both the **elearning_content.png** and
pageheader.png files in the **Project 12** folder. Click
Done. When finished, you can close the Project Log
by clicking the X in the top-right corner.

It might seem odd to remove two files from the
Project Log only to add them right back. The Project
Log tracks all of the frames that have been modified,
however, and these will persist when you begin a new
task. When you add the two files back, notice how
the Frames column has two dashes rather than a
frame number. This means that the files have been
added but Fireworks doesn't remember anything in
particular about the files. In effect, you have given it
a clean slate.

4 Click the Find and Replace tab to return to that
panel. Select Search Project Log from the topmost
drop-down list.

This selection will direct the Find and Replace operation to the files you just added to the Project Log.

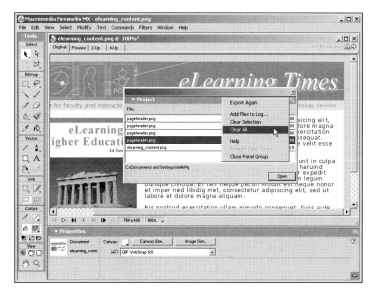

Clear current Project Log
items before beginning
new tasks.

5 Choose Find Color in the second drop-down list. Click the first color button and roll your cursor (which has turned into an eyedropper icon) over a dark area of the banner. The hexadecimal number that appears should be #74695F. When it does, click to select that color.

6 In the second color well, type in **#70A9A9**.

This second number represents the color to which you will be changing the dark background. Leave the default Apply To setting at Fills & Strokes.

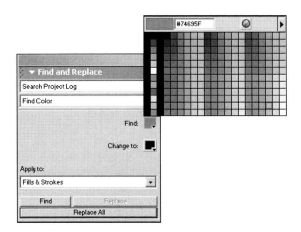

When selecting a color, you can use the swatch pop-up or pull a color from the canvas.

7 Click Replace All. Fireworks makes quick work of all the changes and displays a confirmation window when it is finished.

8 Using the same procedures, replace the current #E7DFD6 color with **#EAF2F2** and click Replace All.

During these Find and Replace processes, Fireworks will quickly open and close your files, so you might get only a quick glimpse at the new color changes being applied.

Note: If you choose to Find and Replace a color and it just so happens that the color appears in some of your bitmaps as well, Fireworks will not alter your bitmaps. Find and Replace operations work only on vector objects—paths, shapes, text, fills, strokes, and effects—not on bitmaps.

9 Switch back to the Project Log. All of the frames of each of the files have their own entry. Again, Shift+select one of each of the files and choose Export Again from the options pop-up menu.

10 In the Export window that appears for each file, use the file's preset settings and click Save. Say Yes to all of the warning pop-ups that notify you that existing files are being overwritten.

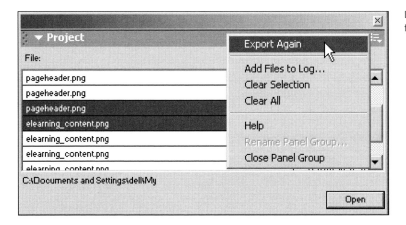

Don't forget to export the files again after the changes.

11 Open any of the HTML files in a browser.

Notice that you have completely changed the color scheme. Of course, Find and Replace won't change the colors of the text (in your HTML file), but if you are using cascading style sheets (CSS), making these changes should take only a matter of minutes.

Note: Changing fonts and color schemes can be combined. That is, after you changed the font, you could have continued with the color changes and only then moved on to the Project Log. In this way, you can make all sorts of changes to multiple files, and the Project Log will track them and simplify the process of re-exporting them.

The original site was just a few commands away from this icy look.

USING BATCH PROCESSING

Working with Find and Replace and the Project Log offers you a variety of powerful tools for automating far-reaching changes to your source Fireworks PNG files. It excels in cases in which you have created whole page designs in Fireworks and in which you have broken these designs into modular components.

If you need to make changes to files that are not Fireworks PNGs, you must use the batch processing utility. In fact, Find and Replace is one of batch processing's capabilities, but many of the commands can be applied to flat bitmaps such as GIFs or JPEGs made in another application.

In this section, you will automate the process of scaling down the four large JPEG photos that appear in the HTML pages.

1 Open Fireworks and close any open files. Choose File | Batch Process.

2 In the Batch window that appears, Ctrl+click (Windows) or Shift+click (Mac) to select the following four files: **parthenon_horiz.jpg**, **selfridges_clock_horiz.jpg**, **sign_post_vert.jpg**, and **statue_eiffeltower_vert.jpg**. Click the Add button to add them to the list of files to process and then click the Next button.

Note: If you can't see the files listed in the window, change the Files of Type option from Fireworks to either JPEG or All Readable Files.

3 In the top-left pane of the Batch Process window is a group of commands. Select Scale and click the Add button to move it to the right pane. The Scale parameters appear.

4 Select Scale to Percentage from the drop-down list of options. Enter **77** in the text field. This setting will scale all four JPEG files that you selected to 77% of their original size.

Note: You can add as many commands as you like to your script and even reorder them. In this project, however, you will only use the scaling command.

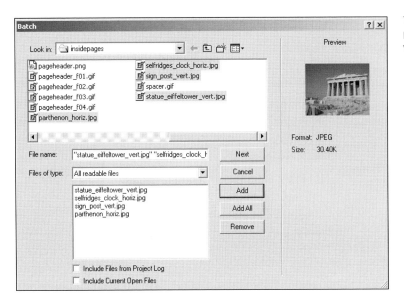

The first step of batch processing is to define which files to change.

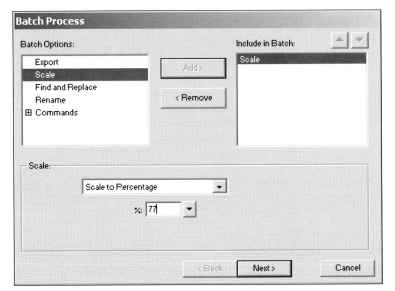

The second step of batch processing is to build the list of commands.

5 Click Next to advance to the third screen of the Batch Process window. This screen lets you specify where to output your batched files and whether you want to back up the originals. (You almost always do.) Check the Backups option if it is not selected already. (By default, it should be selected.)

6 Click the Batch button. Fireworks does the work! An output confirmation pop-up appears when Fireworks is done with the processing. Click OK.

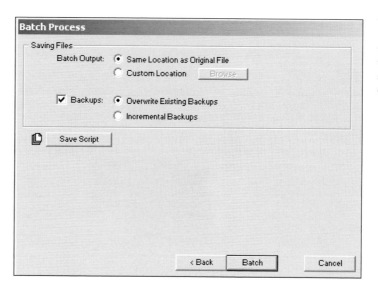

The third step of batch processing is to specify the location of the new files and determine what should happen to the existing files and backups.

7 Now open the HTML files again in a browser. Oddly, the files appear to be the same size, but the quality has degraded. This is because the dimensions of the original image are specified in the HTML <img> tag.

Although the image is now no longer that size, the browser is stretching the image to fit. Unfortunately, this is an HTML issue that Fireworks cannot fix. You need to open each HTML file in Dreamweaver and update the Height and Width attributes.

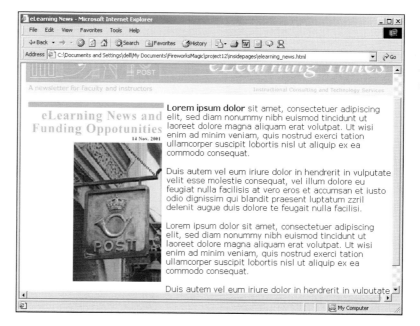

The source image is smaller than before, but following the HTML instructions, the browser is stretching it.

8 Launch Dreamweaver and open all the HTML files in the **Project 12** folder. On one of the HTML files, click the image to select it. In the Properties Inspector, click the Reset Size button to automatically update the sizing information of the image. If you like, right-justify the pictures. Save the file and close it. Repeat this operation for the remaining three HTML files.

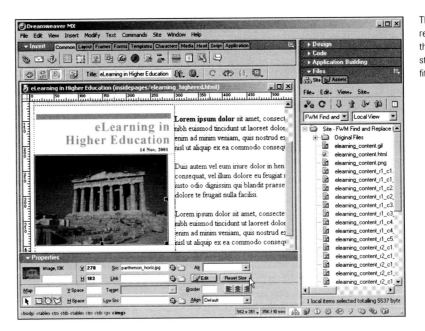

The Reset Size button rewrites the HTML to fit the image rather than stretching the image to fit the HTML.

MODIFICATIONS

The final remaining task is to change each of the frame 2 photos in the nav bar from color to black and white. The Batch Process window has an option to convert images to grayscale. Unfortunately, there is no way that batch processing can affect only selected objects—it affects the whole document. After converting the images to grayscale, you will have to export the images manually by using the Export Selected Slices option.

1 Open the file **elearning_content.png**. Hide the Web layer (if it is visible) and, in the Frames panel, select Frame 2.

When the Web layer is active, it is hard to select objects on the canvas. When working directly with the canvas, you can just toggle it off.

2 While holding down the Shift key, select all four-color photos in the nav bar. You will convert them to grayscale all at once.

3 Choose Commands | Creative | Convert to Grayscale. The four images lose their color.

> **Note:** If you need to enhance the image, use the Adjust Color options in the Filters menu.

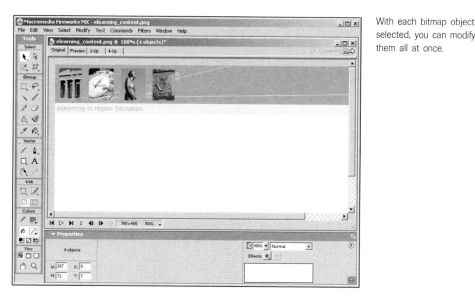

With each bitmap object selected, you can modify them all at once.

4 Return to Frame 1 and turn the Web layer's visibility back on. Select the slice over the first (Parthenon) icon. Right-click (Windows) or Ctrl+click (Mac) and choose Export Selected Slice from the drop-down menu that appears.

5 The now-familiar Export dialog box appears. Be sure that Selected Slices Only is checked and that Current Frame Only and Include Areas Without Slices are unchecked. Click Save. Click OK to the messages about replacing existing files.

6 Repeat this process for the remaining three nav bar slices.

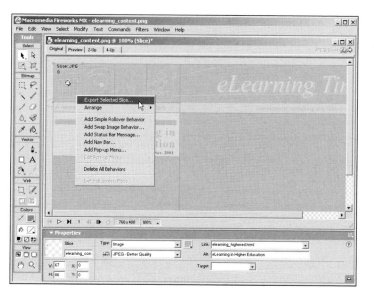

Exporting a selected slice is a quick way to update one portion of a file.

7 Now that you've exported all four images as grayscale images instead of color images, open the HTML files to preview. Your images should now be grayscale.

Preview your final changes in a browser.

AUTOMAGIC GRAPHIC PRODUCTION

"We say we waste time, but that is impossible.

We waste ourselves."

—ALICE BLOCH

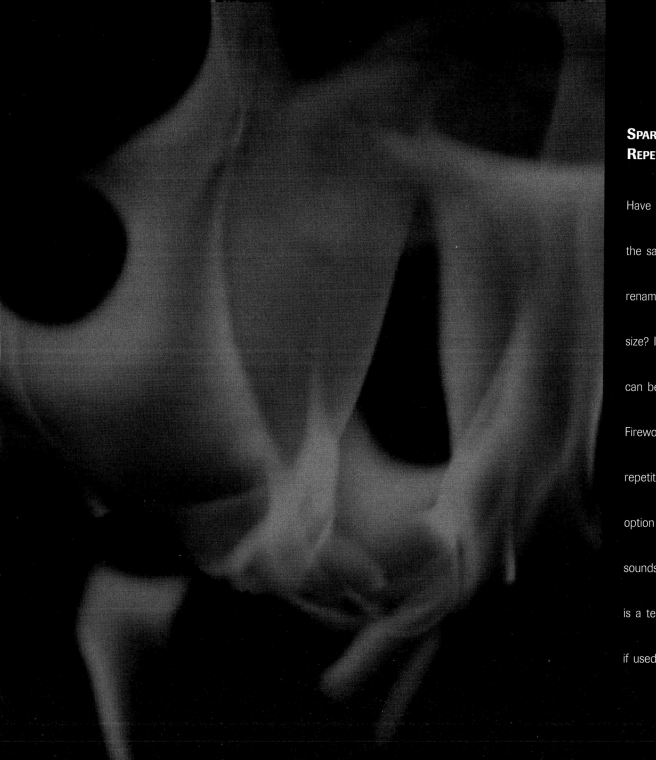

SPARE YOUR BRAIN FROM REPETITIVE TASKS

Have you ever spent an hour or more doing

the same exact thing to multiple files, such as

renaming them or scaling them to a certain

size? If so, you know how tedious a process it

can be and how easy it is to make mistakes.

Fireworks can save you time in completing

repetitive tasks through a little-known window

option called Batch Process. If you think it

sounds boring, you're wrong. Batch processing

is a terrific feature that can save loads of time

if used correctly.

Project 13

Automagic Graphic Production

by Anne-Marie Yerks

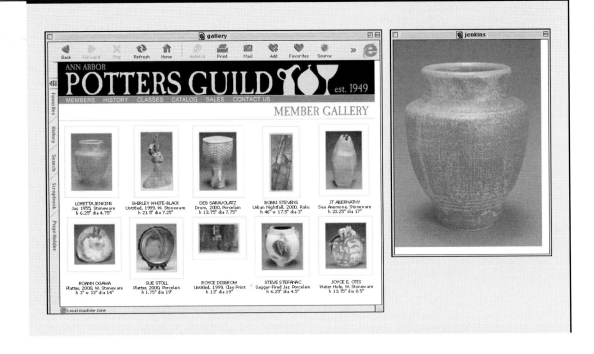

GETTING STARTED

The term *batch process* should be taken literally: If you have a batch of files that all need a certain process applied to them, batch processing will do the trick.

The tasks to be completed should be relatively simple, such as scaling sizes or renaming a set of files. More complicated tasks, namely those that require you to select an object or modify an object inside a file, are not appropriate for batch processing. Batch processing works by running a script that instructs Fireworks as to how to modify a set of files. You are the one who specifies which files (the "batch") should be processed.

To get started, copy the **Project 13** folder from the accompanying CD-ROM onto your computer's hard drive. The image files you need are located in the **guild_tifs** subfolder. It's going to be your job to create an online catalog, converting the images to a web-compatible format (that is, from TIFF to JPEG).

Note: From a web browser, open the **gallery.html** file from the **website** folder (in the CD-ROM folder for this project) to see how the catalog page will eventually look. The first thumbnail image on the page is linked to a larger, more detailed image.

SCALING AND EXPORTING THUMBNAILS

In this section, you will create a set of thumbnail images for a collection of ceramic pots made by members of the Ann Arbor Potters Guild. The images you will work with are TIFFs (Tagged Image File Format), a type of file commonly used in print design. This section of the project will give you experience in scaling and exporting a set of images with the Fireworks batch processing feature. You will use default Fireworks scripts. Later in this project, you will have the opportunity to create your own custom scripts.

1 Open Fireworks and choose File | Batch Process to view the Batch Process dialog box. Access the folder for this project and double-click the **guild_tifs** subfolder. If you are using a PC, change the Files of Type pop-up menu to TIFF. You should see a listing of 15 TIFF files.

No preview is available yet because these images are in TIFF format, which is not compatible with web browsers.

2 Click the Add All button to move the file list into the bottom window. Click Next to move forward.

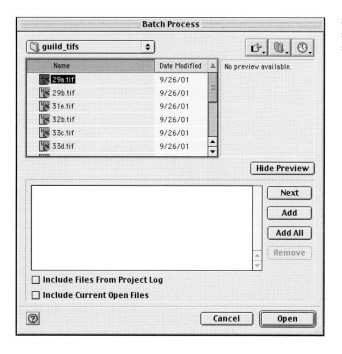

Selecting a folder is the first step in batch processing a set of files.

3 Double-click the Scale option. In the drop-down box at the bottom of the dialog box, choose Scale to Fit Area from the pull-down menu. Enter a Max Width of **90** pixels and a Max Height of **125** pixels.

This option retains the image's proportions, yet keeps them within a specific width and height range of your choosing. This is the best option to use if you want to retain image quality because it doesn't stretch or compress the image vertically or horizontally.

4 Double-click the Export option and choose JPG—Smaller File from the pull-down menu.

This option saves the thumbnails as low-quality JPEGs. By default, Fireworks will assign a 60% quality level, which is perfect for your goal of using all 15 thumbnail images on the same HTML page. Click Next to move to the next window. It's now time to establish the directory into which the thumbnails are to be saved.

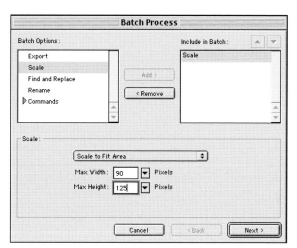

Choose Scale to Fit Area from the pop-up menu to specify the maximum width and height for the thumbnail collection.

5 The **Project 13** folder that you copied onto your hard drive should contain a subfolder called **thumbnails**. To select this folder, click the radio button labeled Custom Location and click the Browse button. Locate and select the **thumbnails** subfolder and click Choose (on a Mac) or select thumbnails (on a PC). The pathname of the **thumbnails** folder should now appear under the Custom Location option. Now it's time to start the batch process.

Note: If you are using a Mac, just select the **thumbnails** folder once before you click Choose. Don't double-click the folder because that will cause you to enter the directory.

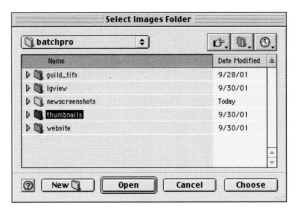

Click the **thumbnails** folder once to select it. Then click the Choose button (Mac) or select **thumbnails** (PC) to designate it as the folder where the batch processed files should be saved.

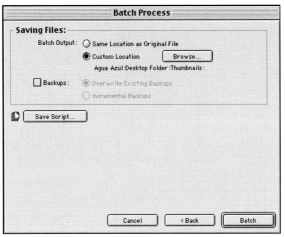

The pathname of the custom folder will appear in the Batch Process window after you have specified your custom location.

6 Click the Batch button to begin. When all files have been attended to, a confirmation window appears. Click the OK button.

After you click the Batch button, Fireworks opens each file and applies the specified commands. The Batch Progress window appears to let you know which file is currently being processed. (This is the time to pat yourself on the back for making the computer do all the pixel pushing for you.)

Click OK to leave the Batch Process dialog box. You can now view the results of your timesaving endeavor.

Note: If you want to apply this same batch process to an additional set of files, click the Save Script button. This button saves your command list for future use. (Be sure to name the command with a .jsf extension.) If you save your script into the **Fireworks MX\Configuration\Commands** folder, it will appear in the Commands menu, where you can use it like any other command.

7 To review your work, choose File | Open. Locate the **thumbnails** folder. You should see a preview of each thumbnail image as you select it. Open one of the files, such as **33d.jpg**.

Note that the images are in JPEG format, which indicates that the files were exported successfully from their original TIFF format. When you open image **33d.jpg** to ensure that the scale operation worked, note that the dimensions are 90×123. This shows that you succeeded. Bravo!

Note: You can also choose Modify | Canvas | Image Size to view the image dimensions.

It's not a bad idea to check the dimensions of every thumbnail in the batch. Of course, you might think this double-checking defeats the purpose of batch processing because it takes up valuable time. But this is a first try, so it pays to check.

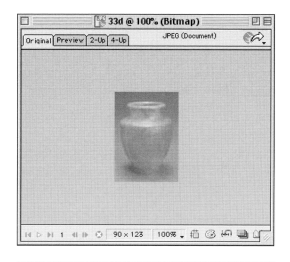

Fireworks displays the image dimensions in the center of the document window.

Note: In this section of the project, you did not create backup files because you put the files into a new folder. If you are saving batch files into the same folder, it's a good idea to check the Backups option so that you don't overwrite your originals.

FRAMING THUMBNAILS

Now that you have created thumbnail images of the ceramics collection, it's time to format the images so that they will look good in the online catalog. The design of the catalog requires that each thumbnail image be framed with thin gray lines. To accomplish this task, you will first need to record a set of actions on one image. This set of actions will be based on the Create Picture Frame command already stored in Fireworks. By saving the recorded actions, you can apply them to the thumbnails folder via the Batch Process dialog box.

In this first step, you will not be performing any batch processing. Instead, you will open a thumbnail image and modify it while recording your actions.

1 Choose File | Open and select the file called **41d.jpg** from the **thumbnails** directory in your project folder.

Make sure the image is not selected.

Later in this project, you'll add a border to the thumbnail images using Fireworks's Batch Processing feature.

2 Choose Window | History to access the History panel.

This panel will list every step you take while creating a frame around the image. Later, you'll use it to save your actions.

3 Choose Commands | Creative | Add Picture Frame. Enter **15** as the pixel width in the dialog box. Click OK.

Fireworks will create a picture frame around the image but will use a default fill. The next task is to modify the frame so that it will meet your design requirements.

4 Unlock the Frame object in Layer 1 and select it. Then, in the Properties Inspector, change the Fill from Pattern to Solid in the Fill pop-up menu and select white as the fill color.

5 In the Effects field in the Properties Inspector, delete the Inner Bevel live effect by selecting it and clicking on the – button.

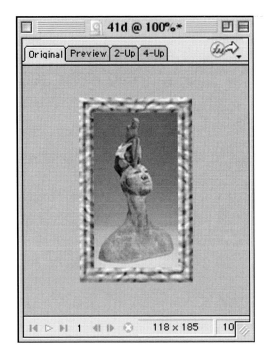

The picture frame will be modified into a simpler design: two gray lines.

6 Change the stroke from None to Pencil | 1-pixel hard in the Stroke pulldown menu on the Properties Inspector. Change the stroke width to **3** pixels. Choose a stroke color of light gray (#999999) by pulling down the color chip next to the Paint Bucket icon. When you have completed these formatting commands, deselect the frame by pressing Cmd+D/ Ctrl+D.

Notice that all of the preceding steps were recorded in the History panel. Each step completed must be saved into a script. You will do that in the next step.

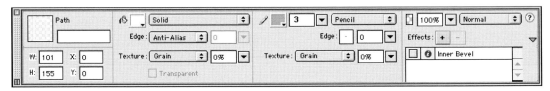

Use the Properties Inspector to format the new frame.

Note: If the framed edges of your thumbnails are getting cut off by the edge of the canvas, you will want to increase your stroke width from 3 pixels to 5 or higher.

7 To save your steps, highlight all the steps listed in the History panel by Shift+clicking each one. When all steps are highlighted, click the Diskette icon located at the bottom of the History panel. In the Save Command dialog box, type **newframe** and click OK.

8 Choose File | Close and don't save the changes.

You will use batch processing to apply the changes to this file again.

9 Choose File | Batch Process. In the Batch Process dialog box, locate the **thumbnails** folder. If you are using a PC, change the Files of Type pop-up menu to JPEG. Click the Add All button to add all the files to the bottom window. Click the Next button.

10 This time, you will work with the Commands option in the Batch Options list. To view the complete list of commands, click the small Plus (+) sign icon in the box next to the word Commands. Scroll down the list of commands that appears, click the Add Picture Frame command, and click Add to place it in the right column. Click on the newframe command and click Add to add it to the right column. Then click the Next button.

11 Click the radio button labeled Custom Location and use the Browse button to choose the **thumbnails** folder as the location for the framed thumbnails. After the directory is chosen, its pathname will be listed in the dialog box. Deselect the Backups option and click the Batch button.

This starts the batch processing. After the batch process begins, Fireworks will open a dialog box for each file, asking you to specify a pixel amount for the width of the picture frame. This is one step that you cannot include in the batch process. Enter a value of **15** each time the dialog box appears. Although this is redundant, the batch process takes care of most of the work for you.

Save the frame with a name you will recognize when it is listed in the Commands menu.

The newly created newframe command now appears as an option under the Commands option in the Batch Process dialog box. It also will appear in the Fireworks Commands menu.

Note: You will not need to worry about overwriting the thumbnail images you created in the first part of the project. A backup set is included in the **backups/guild_tifs** subfolder in the **Project 13** folder.

12 After the batch commands have been applied to every file in the batch, click OK to exit the Batch Processing dialog box.

Tip: Choose Commands | Edit Command List to remove commands from the menu.

You can now view the results of the batch process by choosing File | Open and scrolling through the list of JPEG images in the **thumbnails** folder. Each one is now surrounded with a frame exactly 15 pixels wide. Because the original images from the **guild_tifs** folder had different dimensions, the framed thumbnails are still different sizes. Later, when the images are inserted into an HTML page, each will occupy a table cell of identical height and width.

CREATING A DETAILED VIEW

For this part of the project, you will not work with the thumbnails you created in the preceding sections. Instead, you will return to the original TIFF files in the **guild_tifs** folder. The task in this section is to use batch processing to sharpen the photos and export them as JPEGs in their original dimensions. This new set of larger photos will be used to give users a detailed view when clicking the corresponding thumbnail from the catalog page. Because the close-up image is so important to how users will regard the object, you will sharpen the photos to emphasize the beauty of the pieces.

You also will use batch processing to add a suffix (_large) to the image name. Otherwise, the images would have the same filename as the thumbnails, which could cause problems later when the site is coded in HTML.

Note: On some e-commerce sites, you'll find that the thumbnail image is actually the same file as the larger image; it's just compressed to a smaller size by setting the HTML <width> and <height> tags to a value that is different than the image's true dimensions. This is inefficient not only because it adds bulk to the catalog page (most people don't click on every thumbnail, but the large image would have to load anyway), but also because it causes a loss of quality in whichever image is compressed or enlarged. For the best results, you should use two sets of images as you're doing in this project.

The large-view photos, such as this one, that you create in this section can be linked to the thumbnails created earlier in the project.

1 Choose File | Open and select any of the 15 images in the **guild_tifs** directory in your project folder. (For example purposes, I used the file **33d.tif**.)

2 Choose Window | History to access the History panel.

This panel will list every step you take while sharpening the photo. You'll also use it to save your actions.

3 With the image selected, choose Filters | Sharpen | Unsharp Mask. In the dialog box that appears, adjust the Sharpen Amount to 50.

After you have exited the Sharpen dialog box, the details of the photo should be slightly more apparent. The History palette should now contain a Filter Image command.

4 It's now time to save the steps you've just taken. To do so, highlight the Filter Image command listed in the History panel. If you have more than one step, Shift+click each one to select the entire list. When all steps are highlighted, click the Diskette icon at the bottom of the History panel. In the Save Command dialog box, type **sharpen** (or whatever name you would like to give your command) and click OK.

5 Choose File | Close from the menu and don't save the changes.

You will use batch processing to apply the changes to this file.

6 Choose File | Batch Process. In the Batch Process dialog box, locate the **guild_tifs** folder. If you are using a PC, change the Files of Type pop-up menu to TIFF. Click the Add All button to add all files to the bottom window. Click the Next button.

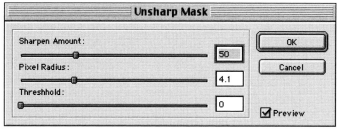

The values shown here will apply a light sharpening effect. Don't oversharpen the photo because doing so causes a loss of image quality.

7 Under Batch Options, double-click Export to include this option in the batch. Do the same for the option called Rename. Now open the Commands list by clicking the Plus (+) sign icon in the box next to Commands and double-click sharpen.

The right column should now contain Export, Rename, and sharpen.

8 In the right column, highlight the Export option. From the Settings pop-up menu at the bottom of the box, choose JPEG—Better Quality.

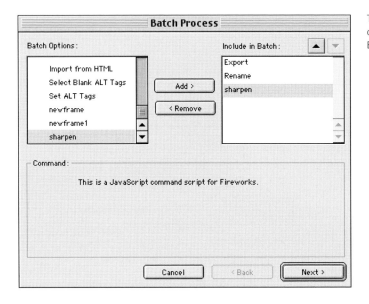

The Include in Batch pane contains the three items: Export, Rename, and sharpen.

9 Highlight the Rename option and choose Add Suffix. Inside the text field, type **_large**. (Don't forget the underscore.)

This suffix will be added to each filename, distinguishing the large photos from the thumbnails. Click the Next button. (Note that there's no need to set properties for the Sharpen command; you already did this when you created the command.)

10 Save your files into the **lgview** folder in the **Project 13** folder you copied to your hard disk. To specify this folder, click the Custom Location radio button and click the Browse button. Locate and select the **lgview** subfolder and click Choose (Mac) or select lgview (PC).

The pathname of the **lgview** folder should appear under the Custom Location option. Make sure the Backups button is *not* selected during this step.

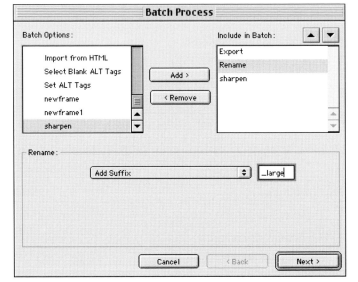

Use the pull-down menu in the Rename area to specify a suffix. The suffix will be added to each file included in the batch.

11 Click the Batch button. Fireworks opens each file and applies the specified commands; you can see what's happening in the background. The Batch Progress window shows you what file is currently being processed. When all files have been processed, click the OK button.

12 After clicking OK, choose File | Open. Locate and open the **lgview** folder. You should be able to view a preview of each image. Note that the images are in JPEG format, which indicates that the files were exported successfully from their original TIFF format. Also note that the _large suffix has been added to each filename.

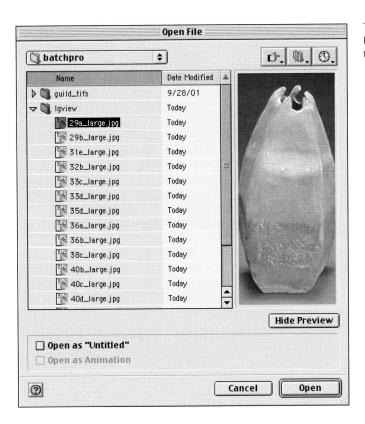

The suffix specified in the Batch Process dialog has been added to each filename.

MODIFICATIONS

The steps taken in this project enabled you to create thumbnail images for a specific site design. However, you could modify these steps for any type of effect you desire. For example, you could create a batch process to change the hue of each thumbnail image. To do this, follow these steps:

1 Apply the Hue filter and save your steps as a command in the History panel. You can then use the command in your batch processes.

Another way to create a photo gallery such as the one created in this project is to use Dreamweaver and Fireworks together.

2 Use Dreamweaver's Create Web Photo Album command to automatically create a set of thumbnails and a set of larger images. First define a site in Dreamweaver using the **Project 13** folder on the hard disk. Then open a new document in Dreamweaver and choose Commands | Create Web Photo Album.

3 Inside the Create Web Photo Album dialog box, select the **guild_tifs** folder as the Source Images Folder and the **thumbnails** folder as the Destination Folder. You can select the thumbnail image size and the number of columns you want to include in the HTML page that Dreamweaver will create.

4 After you click OK, Dreamweaver will open Fireworks and create a set of thumbnails. This set of thumbnails will be presented in a Dreamweaver document, and each one will be linked to its corresponding larger image. Preview the page in your web browser to see if you want to tweak your process at all. Remember to erase the thumbnails from the **thumbnails** folder if you decide to redo the process.

Although the Dreamweaver command will not format the photos with a frame as you did in this project, you can use it to create your initial set of thumbnails and large JPEGs, thereby saving yourself even more time!

These thumbnails were modified with the Filters | Adjust Color | Hue/Saturation command.

Dreamweaver and Fireworks can be used together to create an online photo album. In Dreamweaver, choose Commands | Create Web Photo Album to get started.

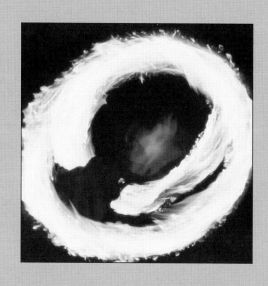

COLLABORATIVE
WORKFLOW

"A brain is like a car: high maintenance,

needs filling regularly, and thankfully

tuning reduces pollution."

—STEVEN GROSVENOR

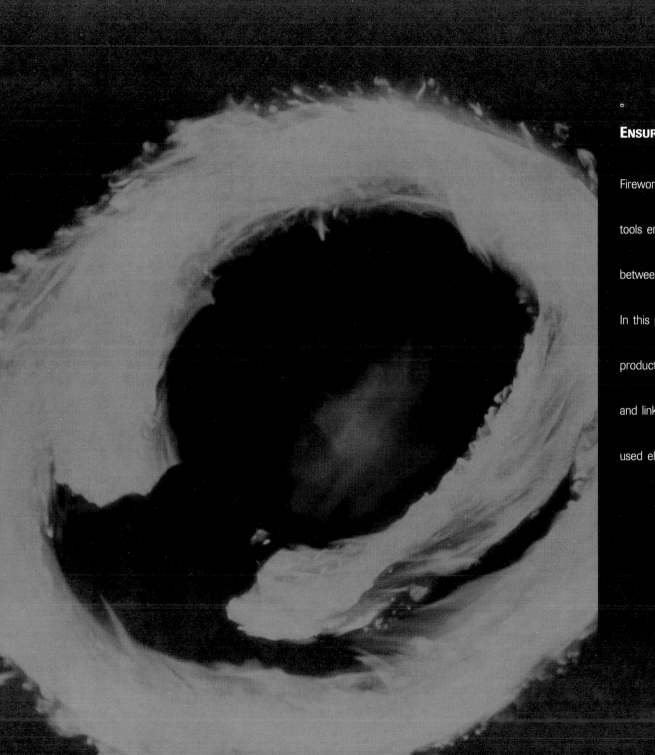

ENSURING DESIGN CONSISTENCY

Fireworks MX extensive collaborative workflow

tools enable easier integration and synergy

between mind, computer, and final production.

In this project, you will learn how to extend your

productivity by using and sharing symbols, styles,

and links to produce, edit, and maintain frequently

used elements within your compositions.

Project 14

Collaborative Workflow

by Steven Grosvenor

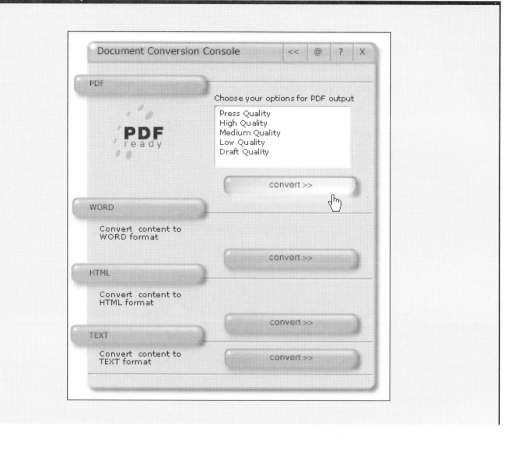

GETTING STARTED

This project shows you how to create reusable, portable web components. You'll first create a few graphics in Fireworks, and then you'll convert them into symbols and styles and learn how to manage them through the Library and Styles panels. The custom styles and symbols you create can then be shared with an entire web team to enhance productivity and ensure design consistency.

Note: So you can concentrate on the methods for using the workflow tools, several portions of the project have been included in the **Project 14** folder on the accompanying CD-ROM. You can work through the project in its entirety, or you can work through specific portions of the project by using the prebuilt files instead.

SAVING BASIC STYLES AND SYMBOLS

By using symbols and styles, you can create design components that are easy to maintain, update, and share with a team. For example, you can create a glassy-looking button and save it as a symbol. You also can save the coloration of its components as graphic styles that you can apply to other objects. By using styles and symbols, a team of designers can maintain a consistent look and feel throughout an entire project.

1 Open **nav_symbol_start.png** from the **Project 14** folder on the accompanying CD-ROM. This file contains the basic background of the navigation symbol, with no effects, symbols, or styles applied.

2 With the Background object selected, apply the following effects from the Properties Inspector.

For the Inner Bevel:

Bevel Edge Shape: Flat

Width: 2

Contrast: 54

Softness: 3

Angle: 135

Button Preset: Raised

For the Drop Shadow:

Distance: 7

Color: #000000

Opacity: 65%

Softness: 4

Angle: 315

3 With the Styles panel open (Window | Styles), click the Plus (+) sign icon at the bottom of the panel to add your effect as a style. Set the following options for the style:

Name: Panel Background (Gray)

Fill Type: Checked

Fill Color: Checked

Effect: Checked

Stroke Type: Unchecked

Stroke Color: Unchecked

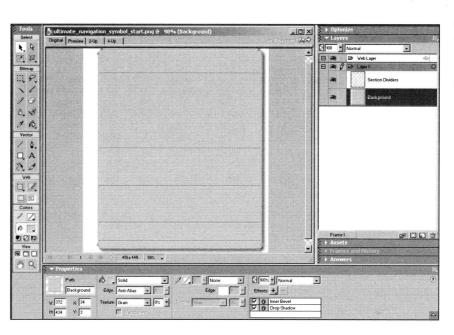

The background for the interface has a subtle bevel and drop shadow effect.

4 In the Layers panel, click the icon next to the **Background** layer to lock this layer. Save this file as **nav_symbol_start.png** to your working directory and close the document.

5 Open the **button_base.png** file. Choose Modify | Canvas | Canvas Size from the menu and enlarge the canvas to 500×500 px. This will give you enough room to duplicate layer elements and relocate them in subsequent steps. Create a new layer named **Swatch** and import **swatch_symbol.png** to this layer from the **Project 14** folder on the accompanying CD-ROM.

6 Select the Base object. Choose the Eyedropper tool and select the top color from the imported swatch, setting the Base object to a rich orange color.

7 Select the Base object and duplicate it. (You can hold down the Option or Alt key and drag a copy of it, or you can choose Edit | Copy | Paste.) In the Layers panel, double-click the copy's name and change it to Base Shadow. Also in the Layers panel, drag the Base Shadow object below the original Base object. Also Shift+ select both of these objects and choose Modify | Align | Left and then Modify | Align | Top to align both objects.

8 In the Layers panel, click to select the Base Shadow object if it's not already selected. In the Properties Inspector, choose Shadow and Glow | Drop Shadow. Use all default Drop Shadow settings but check the Knock Out option to simulate a drop shadow.

9 With the Base Shadow object still selected, from the Styles panel, choose New Style from the Options pull-down menu. Name it **Drop Shadow** and uncheck text-related settings. Click OK.

10 Next select Modify | Symbol | Convert to Symbol. Name the new symbol **Base Shadow** and select the Graphic option. Click OK. Name the Base Shadow symbol **Base Shadow** within the Layers panel.

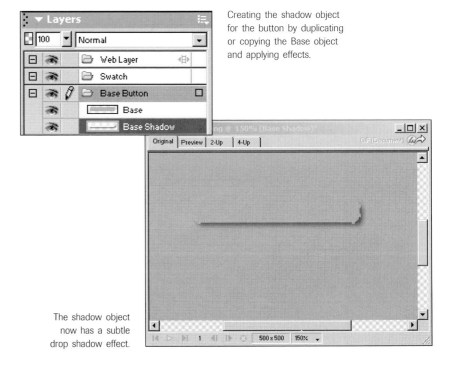

Creating the shadow object for the button by duplicating or copying the Base object and applying effects.

The shadow object now has a subtle drop shadow effect.

11 Click the Eye icon on the Layers panel next to the **Swatch** layer to hide this layer.

12 Now that you've saved a few styles, you should export them as a set that others on the team can use for this project. In the Styles panel, Shift+select the styles you've created so far and choose Export Styles from the Options pull-down menu. Name the file **Master_Styles.stl** and save to your working directory.

13 Save your document as **button_base_final.png**.

Tip: Try to get into the habit of saving your color and gradient choices as styles. Saving a few seconds will eventually add up to hours of saved time!

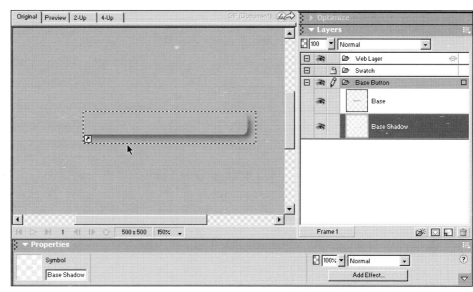

Adjusting the stacking order of the objects to align the shadow object.

CREATING A GLASSY BUTTON SYMBOL

In this section, you'll use various Fireworks drawing techniques to create a glassy-looking button. Because the steps to create a glassy button are fairly complex, it makes sense to save the end result as a symbol that you can share with teammates to ensure the same look and feel.

1 Continue working with your file from the previous section or open **button_base_final.png** from the **Project 14** folder on the accompanying CD-ROM. Select Edit | Clone to clone the Base object and, in the Layers panel, rename it **Highlight Top.** Position it over the Base object on the canvas and within the Layers panel.

2 Select Modify | Transform | Numeric Transform | Scale and set the percentage width and height to 95%, making sure Scale Attributes and Constrain Proportions are selected. Click OK.

3 Set the fill type to be linear (#000000 to #ff6600). In the Gradient Editor, change the opacity of the orange swatch to 0%. Change the direction of the gradient to become vertical by moving the handles so that the square handle is touching the bottom of the path and the round handle is touching the top of the path.

4 In the Properties Inspector, apply the following effects to the Highlight Top object:

Blur | Gaussian Blur: Radius 2

Adjust Color | Brightness/Contrast: Contrast 40

With Highlight Top still selected, convert your coloration settings into a new style by choosing New Style in the Styles panel. Name the new style **Highlight Top**. Now save the object as a symbol by choosing Modify | Symbol | Convert to Symbol. Name the symbol **Highlight Top** and choose the Graphic option. Click OK. Name the symbol **Highlight Top** within the Layers panel.

5 Now that you have created the Highlight Top symbol, create the base glow. Clone the Base object and rename this new object as **Orange Glow**. Place this object between the Base and Base Shadow objects on the canvas and within the Layers panel.

6 Change the Edge Fills from the Properties Inspector to Feather with a setting of 9. Select Modify | Transform | Numeric Transform | Scale and uncheck the Constrain Proportions option. Change the percentage width to 95% and the percentage height to 85% and click OK. Save the object first as a style and then as a symbol named **Orange Glow.** Move the Orange Glow symbol down 7 pixels on the canvas.

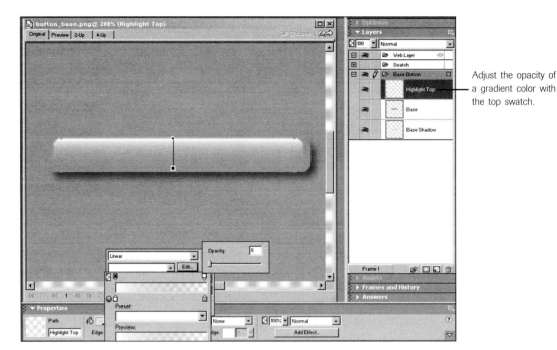

Adjust the opacity of a gradient color with the top swatch.

The button object has a subtle highlight created with the use of transparent gradients.

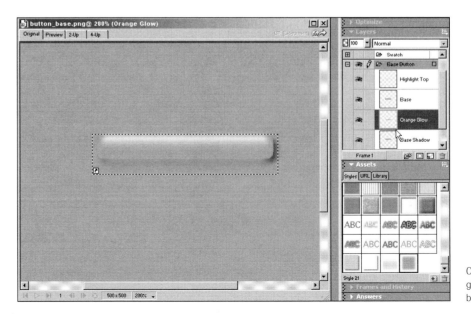

Creating the orange glow object for the button.

7 Clone the Base object twice and make sure the layers are the two topmost layers in the Layers panel. Shift+select both duplicates and use Modify | Align to center them vertically and horizontally to each other. Deselect both.

8 Select the top copy and use the arrow keys to nudge it down 2 pixels and to the right 2 pixels. Shift+select both objects in the Layers panel and select Modify | Combine Paths | Punch. This new shape will act as the top glass refraction layer. In the Layers panel, rename this object **Upper Refraction** and set the fill color to gray (#666666). Add a Gaussian Blur effect of 0.5 pixels and set the opacity of the object to 50%. Save the object as a style named **Glass Refraction**.

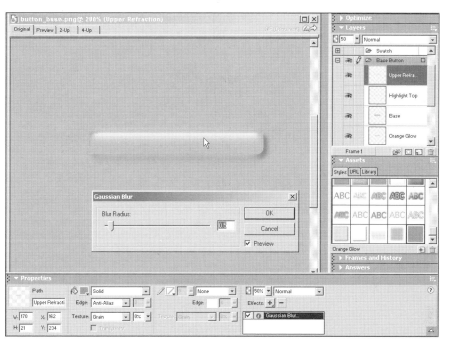

Creating the refraction objects for the button.

9 Duplicate the Upper Refraction object and rename it **Lower Refraction**. Modify | Transform | Rotate the object 180 degrees. Align both the Upper Refraction and Lower Refraction objects with the original Base object so that all three are on top of one another. (You can use the Align panel in the Modify menu to do this.) In the Layers panel, Shift+select only the Upper and Lower Refraction objects and choose Modify | Group. Save the group as a new graphic symbol named **Refraction Group**, naming it **Refraction Group** within the Layers Panel.

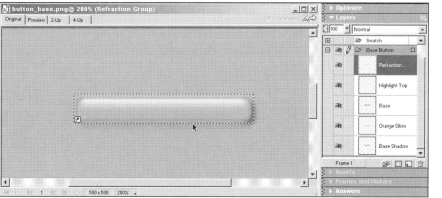

The button now has a subtle glass refraction added to the upper and lower edges.

10 Import **apex.png** from the **Project 14** folder into the **Base Button** layer. Align the imported Apex object with the Base object. With the Apex object still selected, convert it into a graphic symbol named **Apex Artifacts**.

11 Create a 4×4-pixel circle, change the fill color to white, and apply a Gaussian Blur Effect of 1 pixel. In the Layers panel, rename the object **Light Flare** and position it at the top-left corner of the button, making sure this object is the uppermost object in the Layers panel. While selected, save the Light Flare's coloring as a style and then convert it into a graphic symbol named **Light Flare**, naming it **Light Flare** within the Layers panel.

12 To soften up the button's look, add a subtle gradient. Clone the Base object and move to the top of the Layer stack. Set the Fill type to linear (#CC6600 to #FFCC00) and set the opacity of the first color (CC6600) to 40% and the second color (FFCC00) to 0%. Move the gradient handles so that the circular handle is at the top left of the button and the square handle touches the bottom of the button at a 45-degree angle. In the Layers panel, rename the object **Hue Changes**.

13 In the document, move the Hue Changes object on top of the button below the Light Flare object and then convert it into a graphic symbol also named **Hue Changes**. Name the graphic symbol **Hue Changes** within the Layers panel.

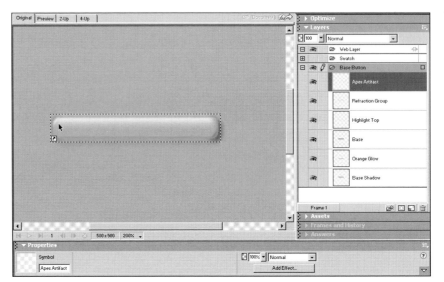

The button now has subtle highlights and lowlights at the apex points.

14 Move the Orange Glow symbol so that it sits between the Apex Artifact and Refraction Group symbols in the Layers panel.

The top left of the button now shows a subtle change in color. (You will see the color change in the CD files.)

Tip: Experimenting with different colors, gradients, and blending methods between objects can produce interesting results.

---

15 Now that you've built a glassy button and have saved its various components as styles and symbols, you can select all of the elements and save them as one Glassy Button symbol. Select all of the objects that make up your button. Choose Modify | Symbol | Convert to Symbol. Notice that a symbol can have other symbols nested inside of it. Name the new symbol **Glassy Button**, check the Graphic option, and click OK.

16 Save your file as **glassy_button.png**.

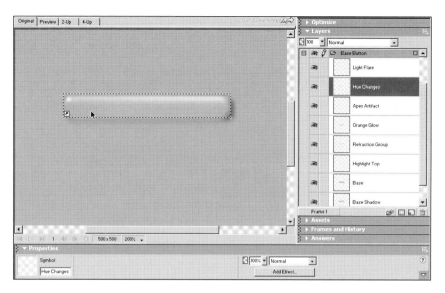

The button components are complete with a softening hue change.

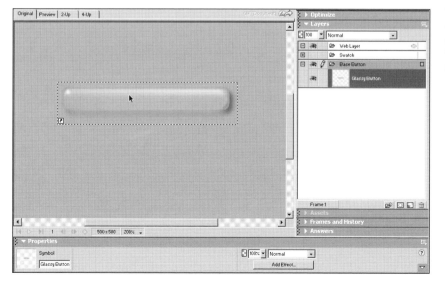

The button component symbols are grouped together as a master symbol.

BUILDING A NAVIGATION BAR

Now that you've built a glassy button symbol, the next step is for you or a team member to build an entire navigation bar with it. By using symbols, you retain control over the look and feel of the design, and updates become a quick and easy process. For example, after you build a navigation bar with multiple copies of the same symbol, you can instantly change the look and feel of the whole navigation bar by making a change to just the source symbol.

1 Start a new document that is 500 high by 400 wide; use the default resolution and set the background color to White. To work with the same Glassy Button symbol that you created earlier, simply import it. Open the Library panel and choose Import Symbols from the Options pull-down menu.

2 Locate the **glassy_button.png** file that you saved earlier or use the one included in the **Project 14** folder on the accompanying CD-ROM. Click Open. A window appears that lists all the symbols for that document. Select the Glassy Button symbol and click Import.

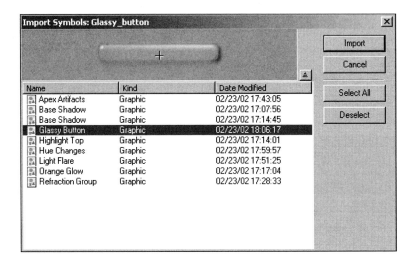

Importing the Glassy Button symbol into a new document.

The Glassy Button symbol, along with the symbols nested within it, will appear listed in the Library panel.

3 Select the Glassy Button symbol in the Library and drag it onto the document, naming the element **First State**. Create a duplicate of the symbol on the page. The original Glassy Button design will become the first state of an interactive button that you'll build. You'll turn the duplicate symbol into the rollover state of the button. To do so, you'll have to break the symbol apart, make changes, and then convert it back into a symbol with a new name.

4 Select the duplicate symbol and choose Modify |
Symbol | Break Apart. The button will now be a
group consisting of multiple symbols. Choose Modify |
Ungroup. Select just the symbols with orange as their
main fill or gradient color and again choose Modify |
Symbol | Break Apart. Now that these symbols are
separated, change the orange to a color of your choice.

5 After adjusting the gradients and fills, remake the
object into a new symbol. Choose Modify | Symbol |
Convert to Symbol. Select the Graphic option and
name it **Button Rollover**.

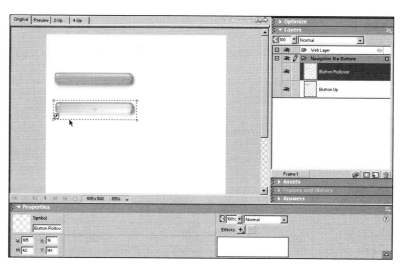

Break apart the
duplicated symbol to
change its coloration.
Save the new design
as a new symbol.

6 Select Edit | Insert | New Button. The Button Editor
window appears, where you can build the Up, Over,
and Down states of a button. Drag and drop the
orange version of your button from the Library panel
into the Button Editor window. Center the symbol in
the window and set both the X and Y registration
points to 0 in the Properties Inspector. Add the text
convert >> (Font: Verdana, Font Size: 10, Color:
#000000) so that it sits centralized in middle of the
button. Now, in the Button Editor, click the Over
tab. Drag and drop the gray version of your button
into the window. Enter the same X and Y locations as
in the orange version. Copy the text you entered in
the Up state of the button to the Over state.

Click Done to close the Button Editor window.

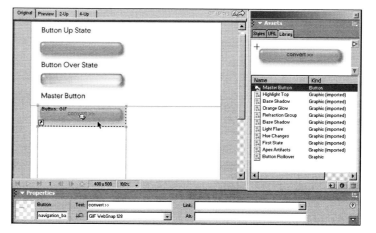

Building the button from a
series of nested symbols.

7 In the Library panel, double-click the new button and rename it **Master Button**. Delete the Up and Over symbols from the canvas and leave only the Master Button. Choose Modify | Canvas | Fit Canvas. Now save the document as **button_source.png** in the **Project 14** folder.

8 Open the **nav_symbol_start.png** file in the **Project 14** folder and add a new layer in the Layers panel. To build a navigation bar using your saved button symbol, you must first import it into the Library panel. In the Library panel, choose Import Symbols from the Options pull-down menu. Locate the **button_source.png** file and click Open. In the Import Symbols window, highlight the Master Button symbol and click Import. The Master Button will now appear in the Library panel, ready for use.

Note that this is the same process that co-workers would go through to use the Master Button symbol in their files.

9 Drag four copies of the Master Button symbol from the Library into your document and position them one above the other in the divided sections.

Voilá! You have an instant navigation bar created from one master button.

10 In the Library panel, choose Import Symbols from the Options pull-down menu. Locate the **interface_pieces.png** file and click Open. In the Import Symbols window, highlight the Interface Pieces symbol and click Import.

The Interface Pieces symbol will now appear in the Library panel. Drag a copy of the Interface Pieces symbol into your document and align so the header fits flush with the top part of the interface.

11 To change the look and feel of the navigation bar instantly, simply change the Master symbol. In the document, double-click one of the buttons. The Button Editor window will appear.

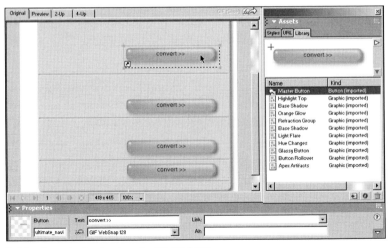

Building the navigation bar from the Master Button.

12 Double-click the symbol in the Up state to open the Symbol Editor window. Because the Master Button is itself a collection of symbols, double-click again. Yet another Symbol Editor window appears. With the Select Behind tool (V) active, keep double-clicking on the orange-colored objects in the Symbol Editor window until you can edit their source paths. Change the color of the fill or gradient from orange to green.

Close all of the Symbol Editor windows to get back to your main document. Your entire navigation bar should now have green buttons!

MODIFICATIONS

What is an interface without functionality? In this final section, you will assign links and URLs to the navigation buttons, bridging the gap between coder and designer. These URLs are fictitious and can be replaced later with URLs of your choice.

1 Open **nav_symbol_final.png** from the **Project 14** folder. From the URL Library panel's Options menu, select New URL Library. Name the library **ultimate_navigation_symbol.htm**.

2 Type the following URLs into the text box and click the Plus (+) sign icon after entering each URL:

convert.asp?type=1

convert.asp?type=2

convert.asp?type=3

convert.asp?type=4

As you enter the URLs, they appear in the box below the entry area.

Adding the links to the button instances within the interface.

197

3 Select Export URLs from the Options menu in the URL Library panel. Name the file **Master_URLS.htm** and save it to a directory of your choice. Now that you've saved your links, you can email them to co-workers so that everyone on the team is using not only the same styles and symbols but the same links as well.

4 Select the first button symbol in the document. Click the first link **convert.asp?type=1** in the URL panel. The link will be assigned to the button. Select the second button and apply the second link. Continue to apply the remaining two links to the remaining buttons. Save your file. To preview your work in a browser, press F12.

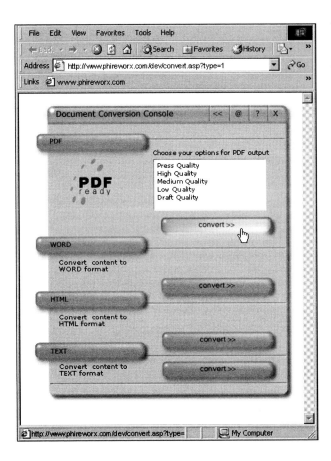

The interface with nested buttons, symbols, and links previewed in a browser window.

POWERFUL FIREWORKS
EXTENSIONS

"One of the great joys in life is accomplishing

what others say cannot be done."

—ANONYMOUS

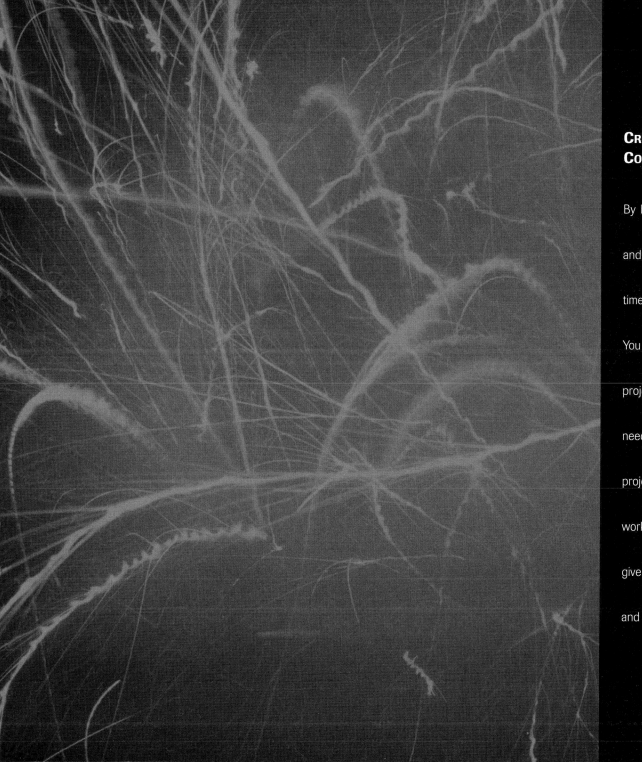

CREATING CUSTOM FLASH-ENABLED COMMANDS

By building Fireworks extensions with JavaScript

and Macromedia Flash, you can save hours of

time when working through repetitive tasks.

You can use these extensions throughout your

projects and can apply them anywhere you

need a productivity or creativity boost. In this

project, you'll look at how Fireworks extensions

work, how they're created, and how you can

give them a nice Flash-based user interface

and share them with others.

Powerful Fireworks Extensions

by Joe Marini

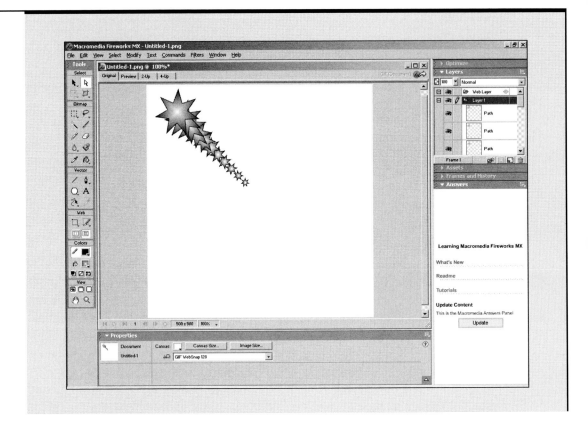

GETTING STARTED

Fireworks extensions are snippets of JavaScript that tell Fireworks to perform certain actions such as creating and manipulating paths, setting colors, moving objects around, and so on. These extensions are accessed from within Fireworks via the Commands menu.

In this project, you'll create a Fireworks extension that simplifies the process of creating an animated series of frames from a given shape. Before you begin creating the actual extension, however, you'll review how Fireworks extensions are created, how they work, and how you can share them with others in your organization or with friends.

To complete this project, you'll need both Fireworks 5 and Flash 5. If you don't have the Macromedia Flash authoring tool, don't worry. I'll show you an alternate way of adding a user interface to your extension.

Fireworks ships with a number of extensions already built in. When you create a new extension, you can access it via the Commands menu. Fireworks extension files are stored in the Commands folder, which is located in the Fireworks MX/Configuration folder. If you look inside the Commands folder, you will see files that end with a .jsf extension. These are Fireworks JavaScript files, and contain the JavaScript code for each extension that you see in the Commands menu. You can share commands with your co-workers and friends by giving them copies of these files. When they place them in their own Commands folder, they will have access to the commands.

When you choose an extension from the Commands menu, Fireworks runs that extension's code, which is stored in the corresponding JSF file in the Commands folder. It is not necessary to surround the code in the JSF file with a <script> tag, as you would in HTML.

The Fireworks Commands menu.

SETTING UP THE DESIGN ENVIRONMENT

In this section, you will set up the Fireworks design environment to create the extension. You'll build a sample document with an object in it that you'll use in creating the extension. You'll then test the extension with the document you've built.

1 Launch Fireworks and create a new document. Give yourself some room to work, preferably 500×500 pixels, a white background, and 72 dpi.

2 In the Vector section of the Tools panel, select the Polygon tool. (You must click and hold the Rectangle tool to reveal the Polygon tool in a pop-up menu.) In the Properties Inspector, select Star from the Shape menu. Set the number of points to 7 and the angle to 45 degrees.

3 Draw a star object in the upper-left corner of the document.

Make the object large enough to work with easily, at least 100×100 pixels.

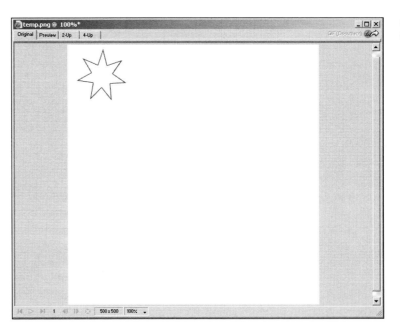

A plain star object on the document canvas.

4 Using the Properties Inspector, select a Starburst gradient fill for the star and select colors of your choice. Select a stroke of 1 pixel.

Your document should now have a seven-point star. Imagine that this simple star element is something you plan to use often throughout a project. Now that you've gone through the steps of building the star, you can save your steps as a custom command. The next time you need a star, you can then simply choose your command from the Commands menu.

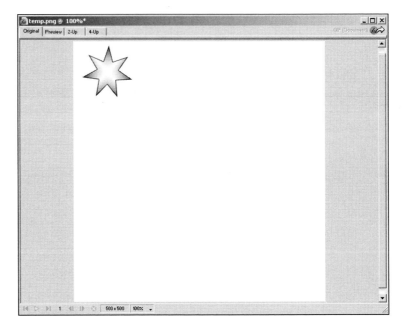

The star object with a Starburst gradient fill.

BUILDING THE EXTENSION BY REMEMBERING A LITTLE HISTORY

Now that you have an object you can work with in your document, let's build the code for the extension. For now, instead of using a text editor, you're going to be using the Fireworks History panel. This provides a list of recent actions that you've taken in the current document and lets you save them as commands.

Each action appears on its own separate line within the panel. Using the History panel, you can select steps and "play" them as if they were a single step. In addition, you can save a set of selected steps as a command. To replay recent actions, you simply select the steps you want to replay and click the Replay button. To save these steps as a command, click the floppy disk icon on the lower-right part of the History panel and enter a name for the command.

1 In the Window menu, select the History panel if it is not already visible (or press Shift+F10).

When the History panel appears, it will likely already contain a list of steps. These are the steps you used to create the star object in the previous section.

> **Note:** The History panel remembers most of the actions you perform in a document, but there are some notable exceptions to be aware of when creating commands. For example, the History panels does not record mouse movements or selections made using the mouse. To capture these events and record them in the History panel, you need to use keyboard shortcuts instead of the mouse.

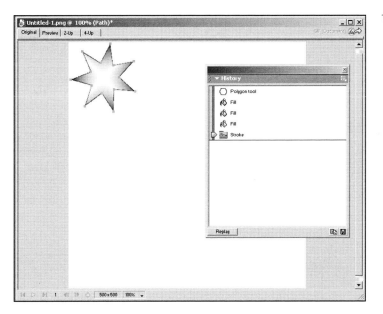

The Fireworks History panel.

2 Because you don't need the original steps, let's get rid of them by clicking on the History panel's pop-up menu and selecting Clear History. Click OK in the dialog box that asks you to confirm your action. Leave the History panel open so that you can watch what happens as you perform the following steps.

3 With the Pointer tool, select the star object in the document you created in the previous section.

4 Clone the selection by pressing Ctrl(Cmd)+ Shift+D. The History panels records a Clone step.

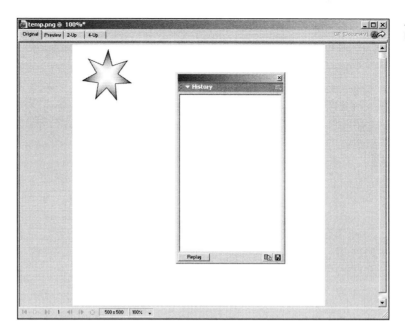

A clean slate—the cleared History panel.

5 Move the selection to the right by holding down the Shift key and pressing the right-arrow key twice. The History panel records two Move steps.

6 Move the selection down by holding down the Shift key and pressing the down-arrow key twice. The History panel records two more Move steps.

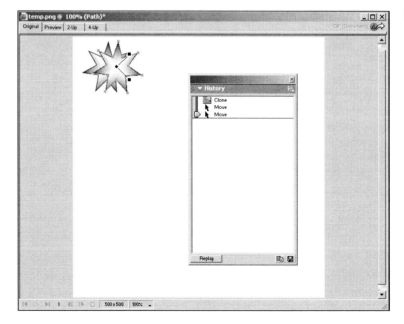

Building a set of History steps.

7 Select Modify | Transform | Numeric Transform. Select Rotate from the Transform Type menu and enter **15** degrees. Click OK. The History panel records a Transform step.

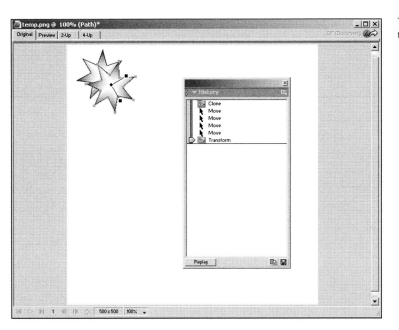

The command takes shape.

8 Select Modify | Transform | Numeric Transform. Select Scale from the transform type menu and enter **80** percent. Leave the Scale Attributes and Constrain Proportions check boxes checked. Click OK. The History panel records another Transform step.

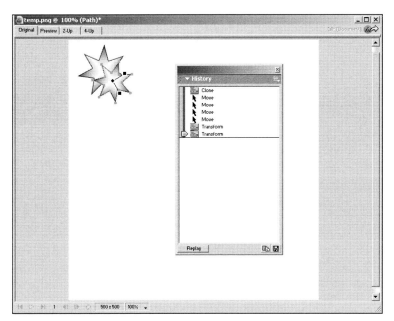

Almost there—all transformations are recorded.

9 Select Modify | Arrange | Send To Back (or press Ctrl+Shift+down-arrow key). The History panel records a Move to Back step.

At this point, the History panel should contain a list of all your steps.

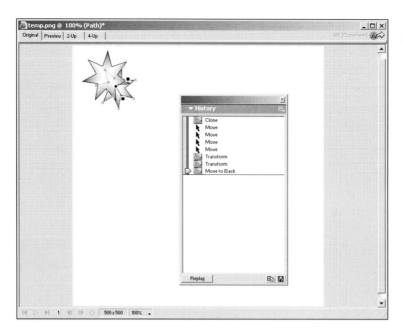

Finished! A complete command built with the History panel.

10 In the History panel, Shift+select the steps you've just recorded and click on the floppy disk icon in the lower-right corner of the History panel. When the Save Command dialog box appears, enter a name for your command such as **My Transformer**. Click OK.

That's all there is to it! Now, if you click the Commands menu, you should see your command listed. You can run this command repeatedly on any selected object or group of objects in the Fireworks document. Note that when you run the command, the History panel records a single Command Script step.

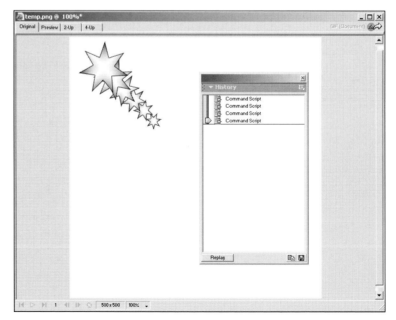

Running the command four times on the star object.

GIVING THE EXTENSION A USER INTERFACE

The command you've created is pretty useful, but it's still narrowly focused. For example, it doesn't let you choose how much to rotate the selected object, how much to offset it each time it is moved, or how much to scale it. The command would be more useful if a user could enter different values for each of these settings instead of having to use the same values over and over again. It also would be great if a user could specify how many times to clone the selection and apply these transformations. The time has come to add a "user interface" to your extension.

In this section, you'll use a text editor to add a basic interface that lets users customize some of the ways your command operates. In the next section, you'll use Flash to add a really snazzy interface to your command.

1   Locate the **mytransformer.jsf** command file you created in the previous section or the **simpleinterface.jsf** file provided in the **Project 15** folder on the accompanying CD-ROM. Open the command file in a text editor like Notepad or SimpleText to see what's inside.

The command file you created from the History panel in the previous section will be stored in the Fireworks MX Commands folder, which is in a different place than in Fireworks 4. It is located in a specific place on your hard drive, depending on which operating system your computer uses (as noted in the following):

```
fw.getDocumentDOM().cloneSelection();
fw.getDocumentDOM().moveSelectionBy({x:10, y:0}, false, false);
fw.getDocumentDOM().moveSelectionBy({x:10, y:0}, false, false);
fw.getDocumentDOM().moveSelectionBy({x:0, y:10}, false, false);
fw.getDocumentDOM().moveSelectionBy({x:0, y:10}, false, false);
fw.getDocumentDOM().rotateSelection(15, "autoTrimImages
➥transformAttributes");
fw.getDocumentDOM().scaleSelection(0.80000001192092896,
➥0.80000000000000004, "autoTrimImages transformAttributes");
fw.getDocumentDOM().arrange("back");
```

Macintosh

- **OS X:** HD/Users/<user name>/Library/Application Support/Macromedia/ Fireworks MX/Commands

- **Classic, single user:** HD/System Folder/Application Support/Macromedia/ Fireworks MX/Commands

- **Classic, multiple users (user):** HD/Users/<user name>/Preferences/Macromedia/ Fireworks MX/ Commands

- **Classic, multiple users (administrator):** HD/ System Folder/Preferences/ Macromedia/Fireworks MX/Commands

Windows

- **98 and ME (single user)**: [Windows directory]\
Application Data\Macromedia\Fireworks MX\
Commands

- **98 and ME (multiuser)**: [Windows directory]\
profiles\<user name>\Application Data\Macromedia\
Fireworks MX\Commands

- **NT**: [Windows directory]\profiles\<user name>\
Application Data\Macromedia\Fireworks MX\
Commands

- **2000 and XP**: C:\Documents and Settings\<user
name>\Application Data\Macromedia\Fireworks MX\
Commands

Note: Some of the code might be familiar to you; some of it might be new to you. Each line of JavaScript code corresponds to one of the History steps you saved in the previous section. The `fw` object is a global object that refers to the Fireworks application. This object enables you to access all the functionality provided by the Fireworks application programming interface (API), a fancy term that means "a bunch of functions you can tell Fireworks to perform." The function `getDocumentDOM()` references your current Fireworks document and the objects it contains.

2 Select and delete all but the first `moveSelectionBy` lines to start consolidating this code.

You don't need four separate calls to `moveSelectionBy()` because you can move the selection both vertically and horizontally in one fell swoop. You can thus consolidate those four lines into one.

```
fw.getDocumentDOM().cloneSelection();
fw.getDocumentDOM().moveSelectionBy({x:10, y:0}, false, false);
fw.getDocumentDOM().rotateSelection(15, "autoTrimImages
➥transformAttributes");
fw.getDocumentDOM().scaleSelection(0.80000001192092896,
➥0.80000000000000004, "autoTrimImages transformAttributes");
fw.getDocumentDOM().arrange("back");
```

3 Create a few return spaces at the top of the code, then add the following line:

The prompt function enables users to change the amount of distance the cloned object is moved each time.

```
var hDist = prompt("Enter a value to move the selection horizontally:");
```

4 Next, add a few more lines that enable the user to control how much the object moves vertically, how much it is rotated, and how much it is scaled.

Notice the names of the variables: `vDist` for how much the object is moved vertically, `r` for how much it is rotated, and `s` for how much it is scaled. You'll reference these variables in the last step.

```
var vDist = prompt("Enter a value to move the selection vertically:");
var r = prompt("Enter a value to rotate the selection by (in degrees):");
var s = prompt("Enter a percentage to scale the selection by (i.e., 90):");
```

5 On the next line, you will add code that will enable the user to repeat the entire command a number of times.

By repeating the command, you will end up with multiple duplicated, moved, rotated, and scaled objects that could comprise the steps of an animation. For example, after running the command, you could select all of the resulting objects and choose the Distribute to Frames option in the Frames panel.

6 On the next line, open a for () loop by adding these two lines:

```
for (i=0; i<count; i++)
{
```

Because you are allowing users to repeat the command, you need to enclose the steps inside of a loop. After the set of commands, close the for () loop with a bracket.

Your final for () loop should look like this:

7 Finally, change the original command code to substitute the variable names (set up in step 4) in place of the hard-coded numbers that were there before.

Your command codes should change to this:

```
var count = prompt("How many times should I repeat?");
var i=0;
```

```
for (i=0; i<count; i++)
{
fw.getDocumentDOM().cloneSelection();
fw.getDocumentDOM().moveSelectionBy({x:10, y:0}, false, false);
fw.getDocumentDOM().rotateSelection(15, "autoTrimImages
➥transformAttributes");
fw.getDocumentDOM().scaleSelection(0.80000001192092896,
➥0.80000000000000004, "autoTrimImages transformAttributes");
fw.getDocumentDOM().arrange("back");
}
```

```
for (i=0; i<count; i++)
{
fw.getDocumentDOM().cloneSelection();
fw.getDocumentDOM().moveSelectionBy({x:hDist, y:vDist}, false,
➥false);
fw.getDocumentDOM().rotateSelection(r, "autoTrimImages
➥transformAttributes");
fw.getDocumentDOM().scaleSelection(s/100, s/100, "autoTrimImages
➥transformAttributes");
fw.getDocumentDOM().arrange("back");
}
```

8 Save your work, go back to Fireworks, and run your modified command on a new object in a new document.

Presto! A configurable command!

Note: Fireworks uses JavaScript just like web browsers do, but there are some important differences you should be aware of regarding how JavaScript is used in Fireworks versus browsers.

First, Fireworks does not embed its JavaScript code inside documents, as browsers do. The JavaScript code is stored separately in JSF files and is called when the user selects a command from the Commands menu. Fireworks also provides support for many more types of objects and functions than regular browser JavaScript does to support features such as selecting objects, working with files, and setting properties of page elements such as transformations and colors.

In addition, when you write JavaScript code for use in Fireworks, don't try to run it in a regular web browser. Chances are good that it won't work, and the browser will display error messages informing you that there are errors in your code.

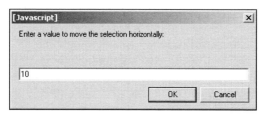

Using the JavaScript prompt function to get values from the user.

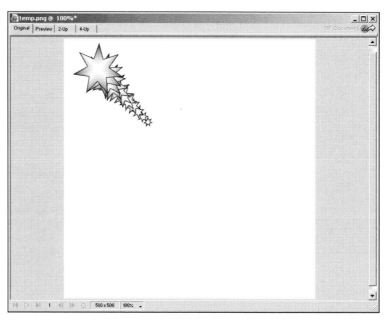

The document after running the command.

MODIFICATIONS

In Fireworks MX, you can now use Flash to give your commands custom user interfaces. When you place a Flash movie into the Fireworks MX Commands folder, it becomes available as a command in the Commands menu.

In the previous section, you gave your command a basic user interface to let users customize your command's operation, but it was pretty cumbersome. The user had to type individual values into multiple dialog boxes, and there was no way to change a value after the user entered it and moved on to the next one. In this last section, you'll fix those problems by using Flash to give your command a more robust interface.

Note: This section assumes you are somewhat familiar with Flash, are able to use Flash to create basic animations, are familiar with ActionScript code, and can attach it to Flash movie objects. If you are not familiar with these concepts, you might not be able to follow the steps, but you will have a chance to see how powerful Fireworks MX has become. Also note that the steps in this section only work with Flash MX, not Flash 5.

1 Launch Flash MX. Open the **scaleandrotate.fla** file included in the **Project 15** folder on the accompanying CD-ROM.

This file is a Flash project that contains the user interface for your Fireworks command. It contains static text items, input text items, and two buttons.

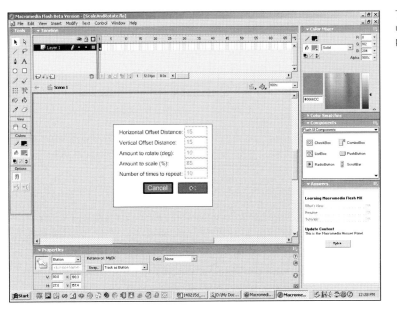

The command user interface project in Flash.

2 Click the Cancel button and choose Actions from the Window menu. The Actions window opens and shows the ActionScript for the Cancel button.

Because the Cancel button simply closes the dialog box without performing any actions, the only script it needs is FWEndCommand(). This function is triggered by the on (release) event handler.

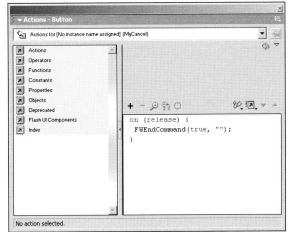

ActionScript code for the Cancel button.

```
on (release) {
  FWEndCommand(true, "");
}
```

Note: Flash MX provides two new ActionScript functions that you can use to communicate with Fireworks: FWJavascript() and FWEndCommand(). You use the FWJavascript() function to execute a string of JavaScript code inside Fireworks. For example, calling FWJavascript("alert('Hello There!');") will cause an alert box to pop up inside the Fireworks application with the message "Hello There!" in it.

The FWEndCommand() function tells Fireworks that the command has completed its work and that the dialog box can close. The function takes two arguments: a Boolean (either true or false), and a text string. To indicate that your command has completed normally and has no errors to report, pass true as the first argument and an empty string as the second argument. If your command has an error condition to report and was unable to complete its work normally, pass false as the second argument and a text string explaining the error as the second. This string will be displayed to the user in Fireworks.

3 Click on the OK button. The Actions window changes to show the ActionScript for the OK button.

Like the Cancel button, you've enclosed your Fireworks code inside an `on (release)` button handler. The difference here, however, is that you've taken the code generated from the History panel in the previous section and broken it up into multiple lines. All of the `prompt()` functions have been removed because the values for the command will now come from the interface's text fields. The text fields have been named so that you can refer to them in the ActionScript.

> **Tip:** Each line of code is broken up into a separate call to `FWJavascript()`, but you could have simply built all of it as one giant text string and handed it all to Fireworks at once. The reason for making each line a separate call is to better aid in debugging. If the command is causing problems or not working properly, it is easier to comment out individual lines to determine which one is causing the problem.

4 Export the movie by selecting Export Movie from the File menu. Name the movie **scaleandrotate.swf**. Save the SWF file in your Fireworks MX/ Configuration/Commands folder.

5 Start Fireworks, create a new document, and draw a simple circle object with the Shape tool.

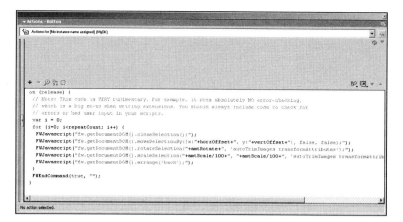

ActionScript code for the OK button.

6 Select the Scale and Rotate command from the Commands menu. When the dialog box appears, enter different values in the input text fields and click OK.

Watch how your Flash-enabled command whirls and twirls your design!

Note: As a precaution, click in each text field to enter the data as opposed to using the Tab key to move from field to field. Otherwise, the interface might crash.

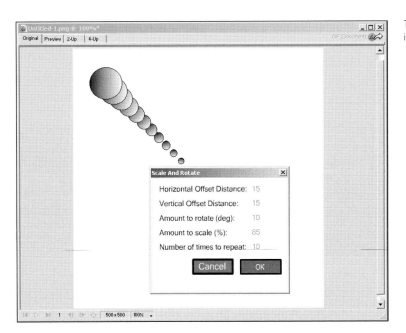

The Flash command in action.

INDEX

mastheads, 33
merging, 56
  viewing seams, 56-57
pasting inside other images, 26-28
removing the fringe, 22
repairing after adjustments, 21-22
resizing, 26
rotating, 20, 30
stretching, 24
web banners, 29
Blending mode (layers), 25
Blur tool, 56
browsers, use of JavaScript in, 212
Brush tool, 55-56
buttons
animations, triggering, 67-70
creating, 186-188
glassy-looking, 189-193
  saving as symbols, 193
graphics, creating, 116-118
links, adding, 122
logo, 92
  animated Down states, 99
  creating, 93-94
  exporting, 96-97
  importing into Flash, 97-98
  rollover effects, 93
navigation bars, 116
  links, assigning, 197-198
navigation bars, creating, 194-197
rollover, 37, 67-68
  rollover states, creating, 67
symbols
  creating, 118-120
  navigation bars, building, 120-123
  saving as, 188
bylines, animated, 37

C

canvases, enlarging, 55
centering text in buttons, 119
Circle tool, 93
circles, drawing, 93-95
collaborative workflow, 185-186
styles and symbols, saving, 186-193
collages
creating, 18
uses of in web sites, 28-33
color
adding to illustrations, 8-10
in buttons, 120
fill colors, changing, 67
fill gradients, 8, 12
  changing position, 27
  custom fill patterns, 14-15
  Radial gradients, 27
matte colors for background tiles, 59
schemes, changing, 160-162
  exporting changes, 162-163
text, 120
commands
configurable, 209
custom, 208
  storing, 209
  user interfaces, 209-212
repeating, 211
composite images
creating, 18
in web sites, 28-33
Configuration folder, 57
**Create Web Photo Album command
  (Dreamweaver), 182**
Crop tool, 150

D

delay, interframe, 70
design consistency, 185-186
styles and symbols, saving, 186-193
designs
exporting, 37-38
  slicing, 38-40
optimizing, 37-38
  slicing, 38-40
updating, 155-157
disjoint rollovers, 38, 77
drawing with shapes, 5-7
intersecting shapes, 7
Dreamweaver
Create Web Photo Album command, 182
Fireworks, integrating with, 141-142
  behaviors, applying, 143-145
  editing, 147-149
  exporting elements individually, 150-152
  exporting interfaces, 145-147
  slicing, 143-145
HTML tables, nesting, 42
text, formatting, 143
tiles
  as backgrounds in table cells, 62
  embedding in web pages, 61
drop shadows, 74, 117

E

editing
files, optimizing for use with Dreamweaver, 147-149
HTML, 109
effects
Drop Shadow, 74
Swirl Filter (Alien Skin), 28
Ellipse tool, 60, 117
Export Area tool, 49, 59

automating changes across a series of files, 157-160
batch processing, 163-168
color schemes, changing, 160-162
exporting changes, 162-163

URL panels, 107, 144

links
    adding to URL libraries, 108
    applying to web pages, 108-109
custom behaviors, adding, 149
exporting link libraries, 111
HTML files, importing as lists of links, 107
link libraries, creating, 107
link libraries, updating, 110
    across multiple documents, 111-112

user interfaces

custom commands, 209-212
custom, creating with Flash, 212-215

utilities

Blur tool, 56
Brush tool, 55-56
Circle tool, 93
Crop tool, 150
Ellipse tool, 60, 117
Export Area, 59
Export Area tool, 49
Eyedropper tool, 188
Freeform tool, 11
Hand tool, 44, 49
Knife tool, 80
Lasso tool, 41
Magic Wand tool, 22
Marquee tool, 19, 24, 27, 56
Pen tool, 5-7, 80
Pointer tool, 7, 55, 57, 118, 206
Polygon Lasso tool, 20-21
Polygon tool, 203
Rectangle tool, 25, 27, 58, 116
Reshape Area tool, 117
Rounded Rectangle tool, 31, 79
Rubber Stamp tool, 18, 22
    pointers, 22
    using without making selections, 22

Scale tool, 20, 80, 94-95
Selection tools, 18
Shape tool, 5, 214
Slice tool, 39, 68, 143
Subselection tool, 80-81, 95
Text tool, 82, 118-119
Transform tool, 100

vector tools, creating button graphics, 116-118

W-Z

web banners, 29

web sites

previewing in browsers, 113
updating
    automating changes across series of files, 157-160
    batch processing, 163-168
    color schemes, changing, 160-162
    exporting changes, 162-163
    graphics with batch processing tools, 155-157

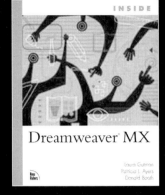

VOICES THAT MATTER

VISIT OUR WEB SITE

WWW.NEWRIDERS.COM

On our web site, you'll find information about our other books, authors, tables of contents, and book errata. You will also find information about book registration and how to purchase our books, both domestically and internationally.

EMAIL US

Contact us at: **nrfeedback@newriders.com**

- If you have comments or questions about this book
- To report errors that you have found in this book
- If you have a book proposal to submit or are interested in writing for New Riders
- If you are an expert in a computer topic or technology and are interested in being a technical editor who reviews manuscripts for technical accuracy

Contact us at: **nreducation@newriders.com**

- If you are an instructor from an educational institution who wants to preview New Riders books for classroom use. Email should include your name, title, school, department, address, phone number, office days/hours, text in use, and enrollment, along with your request for desk/examination copies and/or additional information.

Contact us at: **nrmedia@newriders.com**

- If you are a member of the media who is interested in reviewing copies of New Riders books. Send your name, mailing address, and email address, along with the name of the publication or web site you work for.

BULK PURCHASES/CORPORATE SALES

If you are interested in buying 10 or more copies of a title or want to set up an account for your company to purchase directly from the publisher at a substantial discount, contact us at 800-382-3419 or email your contact information to corpsales@pearsontechgroup.com. A sales representative will contact you with more information.

WRITE TO US

New Riders Publishing
201 W. 103rd St.
Indianapolis, IN 46290-1097

CALL/FAX US

Toll-free (800) 571-5840
If outside U.S. (317) 581-3500
Ask for New Riders
FAX: (317) 581-4663

New Riders

Solutions from experts you know and trust.

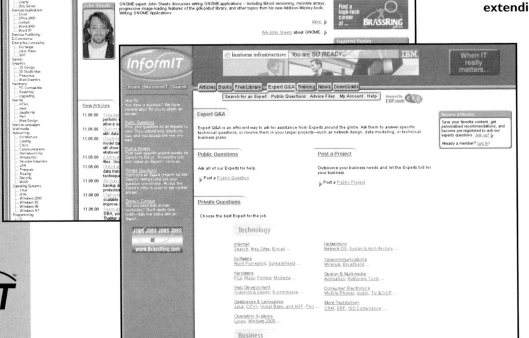

Publishing
the Voices
that Matter

OUR AUTHORS

PRESS ROOM

| web development | design | photoshop | new media | 3-D | server technologies |

EDUCATORS

ABOUT US

CONTACT US

You already know that New Riders brings you the **Voices that Matter**. But what does that mean? It means that New Riders brings you the Voices that challenge your assumptions, take your talents to the next level, or simply help you better understand the complex technical world we're all navigating.

Visit **www.newriders.com** to find:

▸ Discounts on specific book purchases

▸ Never before published chapters

▸ Sample chapters and excerpts

▸ Author bios and interviews

▸ Contests and enter-to-wins

▸ Up-to-date industry event information

▸ Book reviews

▸ Special offers from our friends and partners

▸ Info on how to join our User Group program

▸ Ways to have your Voice heard

New
Riders

WWW.NEWRIDERS.COM

WHAT'S ON THE CD-ROM

The accompanying CD-ROM is packed with all sorts of exercise files and products to help you work with this book and with Fireworks. The following sections contain descriptions of the CD-ROM's contents.

For more information about the use of this CD-ROM, please review the **readme.txt** file in the root directory. This file includes important disclaimer information as well as information about installation, system requirements, troubleshooting, and technical support.

> **Technical Support Issues:** If you have any difficulties with this CD-ROM, you can access our web site at **www.newriders.com**.

SYSTEM REQUIREMENTS

This CD-ROM was configured for use on systems running Windows 98, Windows 2000, Windows XP, and Macintosh. Your machine will need to meet the following system requirements for this CD-ROM to operate properly:

- Macintosh OS System 9.1 and above
- Windows 98 and above

LOADING THE CD-ROM'S FILES

To load the files from the CD-ROM, insert the disc into your CD-ROM drive. If autoplay is enabled on your machine, the CD-ROM setup program will start automatically the first time you insert the disc. You can copy the files to your hard drive or use them right off the disc.

> **NOTE:** This CD-ROM uses long and mixed-case filenames, requiring the use of a protected mode CD-ROM driver.

EXERCISE FILES

This CD-ROM contains all the files you'll need to complete the exercises in *Fireworks MX Magic*. These files can be found in the root directory's project folders.

READ THIS BEFORE OPENING THE SOFTWARE

By opening the CD-ROM's package, you agree to be bound by the following agreement:

You may not copy or redistribute the entire CD-ROM as a whole. Copying and redistribution of individual software programs on the CD-ROM is governed by terms set by individual copyright holders.

The installer, code, images, actions, and brushes from the author(s) are copyrighted by the publisher and the authors.

This software is sold as-is without warranty of any kind, either expressed or implied, including but not limited to the implied warranties of merchantability and fitness for a particular purpose. Neither the publisher nor its dealers or distributors assumes any liability for any alleged or actual damages arising from the use of this program. (Some states do not allow for the exclusion of implied warranties, so the exclusion may not apply to you.)